I0438778

SINGLISM

An Intelligent Answer
to the
Singularity that Is

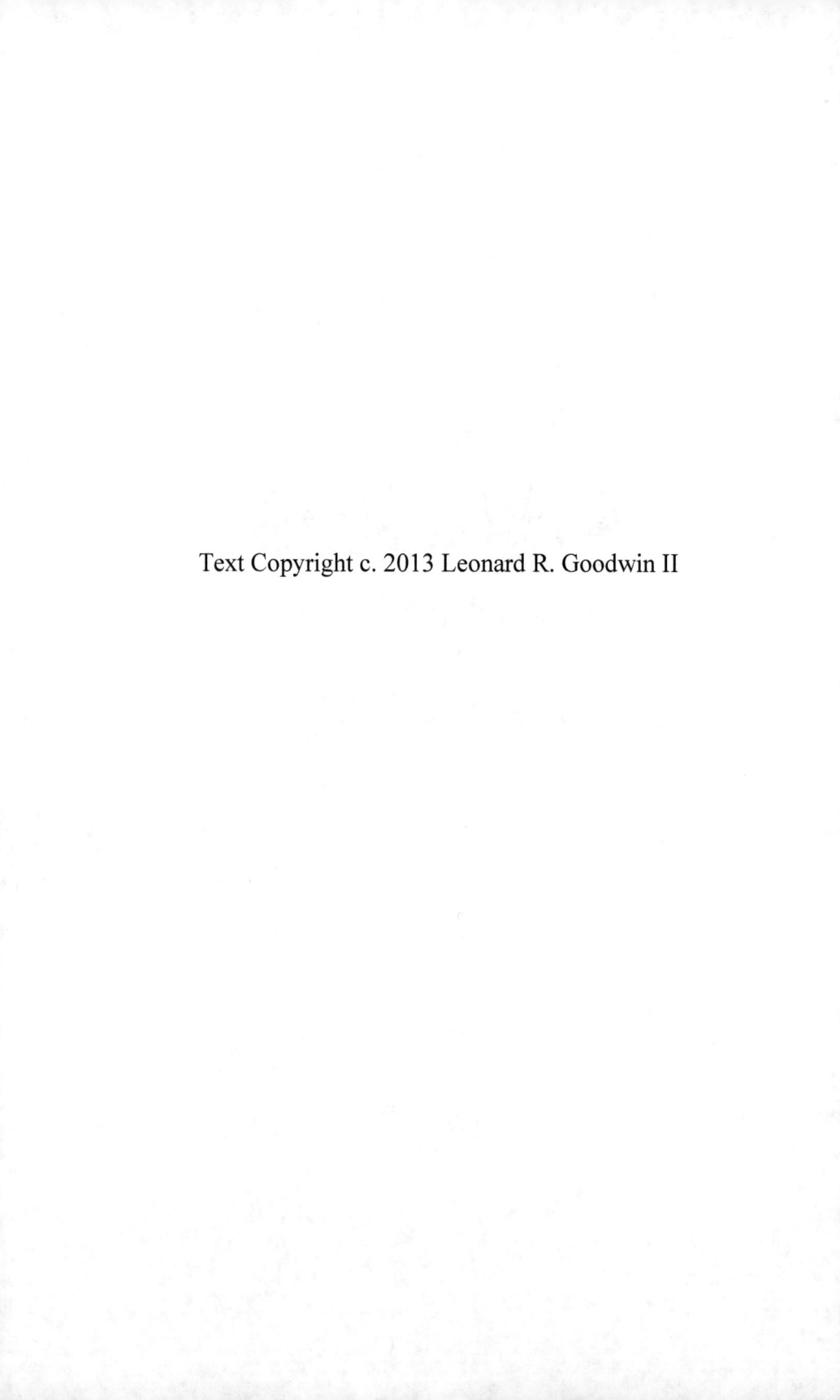

Text Copyright c. 2013 Leonard R. Goodwin II

To my Carmen Ann
for her extreme patients
with me.

Table of Contents

Chapter 1 Singularity

Chapter 2 Human Rights

Chapter 3 Economy

Chapter 4 Transition

Chapter 5 What do we gain?

Chapter 6 Freedom

Chapter 7 Energy!

Chapter 8 Connectivity and Laws

Chapter 9 Realities!!!

Chapter 10 Healthcare

Chapter 11 Education

Chapter 12 More Education

Chapter 13 Almost There?

Chapter 14 Transportation

Chapter 15 Transition

Chapter 16 God and Religion

Chapter 17 Goals

Chapter 18 Future

Who I am?

Addendum

Forward

This text is a blueprint for a new world. A world that we can and must create. If we fail to create a new world, then we are doomed to die on a planet stripped of it's resources. A planet scared by endless wars, a planet with no life on it other than the last holdouts of mankind. We will doom ourselves and our children to the nuclear holocaust that we have feared for so long. In the following text the chapters may be labeled as one subject or another, but a chapter may discuss any number of subjects. I truly hope that you all listen. I am charging for the first copy, but feel free to print that copy and give it away. Everyone on the planet needs to read this text. I assume that it will be banned in every other country on the planet in a matter of months. I actually hope that it will be banned as no book is more read than one that has been. Thank you LRG II

Chapter 1 Singularities

Answers or Questions?

I want to start with the definition of a singularity and what that means in context with this text.

But before we start, look around you. Are you happy? Are you stressed? Do you like what you do for a living? Do you look forward to getting out of bed? Do you feel the angst that underlines our world today? Have you seen the thousands of documentaries that tell you how bad the world is? Do you worry about fresh water? Do you worry about chemicals in your food? Do you worry about BPA in your water bottles? Do you worry about global warming? Do you worry about instability in the Middle East? Do you think your country is headed in the right direction? Do you think that we are on the precipice? Do you believe that we are living in the end times? Do you think we can save the planet? Do you think we can save the human race? Do we deserve to be saved?

Have you heard anyone say, "Here, right here is the

answer to it all?" No! Well, if you will give me a few hours of your time and open your mind, I will tell you how we can save the planet and ourselves at the same time. There are two paths, the one we are on and the one I am about to show you. Singlism is the answer. I hope the world listens.

   Let us begin with the mundane, I have a reason for wanting you to read it, so……..

Singularity as defined by wikipedia,

> *İMathematical singularity, a point at which a given mathematical object is not defined or not "well-behaved", for example infinite or not differentiable.   Singular point of a curve, where the curve is not given by a smooth embedding of   a parameter. Singular point of an algebraic variety, a point where an algebraic variety is not locally flat. Rational singularity, a concept in singularity theory. Singularity theory, which deals with these concepts. Essential singularity, a singularity near which a function exhibits extreme behavior. Isolated singularity, a mathematical singularity that has no other singularities close to it. Movable singularity, a concept in singularity theory. Removable singularity, a point at which a function is not defined but at which it can be so*

defined that it is continuous at the singularity. Gravitational singularity, a point in spacetime in which gravitational forces cause matter to have an infinite density and zero volume. Mechanical singularity, a position or configuration of a mechanism or a machine where the subsequent behavior cannot be predicted. Penrose–Hawking singularity theorems, theorems in general relativity theory about when gravitation produces singularities such as black holes. Prandtl–Glauert singularity, the point at which a sudden drop in air pressure occurs. Singularity (climate), a weather phenomenon associated with a specific calendar date. Van Hove singularity in the density of states of a material. Technological singularity, is a theoretical moment in time when artificial intelligence will have progressed to the point of a greater-than-human intelligence. The Singularity Is Near, a 2005 non-fiction book by Ray Kurzweil. Singularity (operating system), an operating system developed by Microsoft Research written in managed code.

In Literary studies,

*Temporal singularity, otherwise knows as a _point of_*
divergence, a concept in _speculative fiction_, usually an item
or event triggered by an item that results in divergent
narratives, in which the singularity alters the new timeline
away from a prior "default" state, leaving behind a parallel
universe in which the singularity did not occur. This is the
basis of much of the _Alternate history_ genre. It may involve
technology in "hard" science fiction, or may involve anything
up to or including magic as the basis of the "what if?"
scenario.

The Singularity, or one of its iterations, can be found throughout science fiction and popular culture, but after reading the above definitions combined with your personal perception, can you tell me what it is? Would you recognize a singularity if one occurred in front of you? Scientists are waiting for the singularity to "converge" within the confines of our technology. (They expect it to happen within the next ten years, I expect it in less than two.) Scientists, technologists, science fiction writers and futurists believe that a computer's hardware systems will combine with it's software to create an all aware intelligence. By definition, is that "singular"? What is missing in science, or it's varied fictions, is the obvious, "Humanities Singularity"!

Humanities Singularity? We, as a race have reached our singularity! It's what we, as a race, have been working toward for the last quarter of a million years. What could I possibly mean by this? To me, it's obvious, I hate to try to explain it. It's so simple after all. Where does a person start when he has to explain a "simple" idea. Let's start with what you would think is obvious.

All of humanity has the right to exist in harmony with their family, within their community, within their country. All of humanity has the right to the resources required to live a happy and healthy life. All of humanity has the right to a proud, private and comfortable home. All of humanity has the right to a pristine environment. All of humanity has a right to worship as it suits them, or not. All of humanity has a right to an unadulterated, non-toxic, healthy and plentiful food and water source. All of humanity has the right to choose who they care about, who they want to make a part of their family and a part of their home. Just to make sure we cover everything that every human has a right to, lets use the United Nations Declaration of Human Rights as an addendum to this text so I will add it to as an addendum.

Nice, right? All of these rights? Communism, you scream? No, not communism, Singlism? Unachievable, you say? No. We live in a time (thank your local multinational) where our warped version of Darwin competitiveness has driven us to build a world wide infrastructure that we can "un-build" on. Where we can use the tools developed over centuries to make the world a truly wonderful place for all of us to live. O.K? What's to stop you from saying, "B.S." and laying down this text and never picking it up again? Well, for that, I want your imagination for a few minutes. Dream, dream of what could be, what will be, what will cost us dearly to achieve. I assume that I will be killed for writing this. Why? Too utopian? No, too realistic.

Forget conservatives, liberals, socialists, communists, capitalists or any other "ists". Now is the time for singlism. Singlism, which I base on humanity having the ability to institute a hive mind. A singular cooperative among people based on family, home, community, district, city, county, state, country and nation. The problem with the current political systems, (ALL POLITICAL SYSTEMS) is they only pay lip service to the people. They are all based on cash and resources and skewed through the lenses of nationalism. This is one of the first things that must be changed before anything can be accomplished.

Chapter 2 Human Rights

I started with our rights as humans, correct? Have you ever read the U.N's Universal Declaration of Human Rights? It says everything that I won't and I agree with almost the entire thing. What Human Right are you against, you say? Article 17, the right to own property, I think you have the right to own your home. The earth and every square foot of land, the resources derived from it belong to everyone. Article 17 is therefore amended to the right to own PERSONAL property. Just because your ancestor fell into a hole and found gold, it belongs to your family alone? All resources for all people! You have the right to own your personal possessions and your home is sacred. Your family is sacred.

I have a problem with Article 30 as well, which basically states that we have decided that you have these rights. However, don't you dare fight for your rights because you might actually deprive the oppressors of their rights! Right? I believe that's the jist of what it says. Actually, it says that the declaration doesn't allow for any state or any other entity to commit any act which would deprive another of their rights. It sounds good, like no one is allowed to deprive you of your rights. Strange, if it wasn't making such an implication, why add that Article in the first place. Shouldn't the right not to be deprived of rights, be a given? Starting to get a headache here.

What I believe Article 30 should say is, "If a state or other entity should try to deprive anyone of any of their rights, they shall be banned from the earth forever!" Which, once again is a given. We should not have to declare that our rights are our rights and that we have the right to defend those rights even if they deprive the oppressor of their rights. Does that even come close to making sense? I digress.

Which brings me to my next point, families know how to talk to one another, just as districts, countries etc. know how best to communicate amongst themselves. Local control means local laws which means local language enforced by local people. Self-policing will start within the family itself. Oversight will be structured along the same lines as the council system laid out ahead. I do have one other thing to say about policing organizations, no one should be allowed to enforce the laws of a country unless they have received formal approval of the family/district/state council of it's origin. No one in this profession should be younger than thirty-two.

I have a problem with the United Nations itself, they exist for the rights of Nations, not for the rights of the people. Their entire existence is to legitimize the "Nation State." Nation States are a divider of peoples. The United Nations is a divider of people. The last thing the people who work in the U.N. want is cooperation among the peoples of the world. Tough, that's where we're going, without the U.N. of course. It is an extravagant waste of resources. What little HUMANITARIAN aid they distribute every year is outweighed by the back room deals to sell and trade the resources of one country for the benefit of another. (Note: The U.N. Universal Declaration of Human Rights is attached as an addendum to this text.)

Now that we have discussed the "rights" of man. I have to get to the "bones" of the plan. Every family on the planet will have a home to be proud of. Every family will have the food and resources they need to live a happy healthy life. They will have clean water and unadulterated food. They will live in concentrated self sustaining "cities" where they can live and work in peace with their fellow neighbors. Every human will be "plugged" into a digital system that allows them to live two lives. One will be their physical life, the second will be their DS or digital self. I will expand on all of this further if you will give me the chance to explain. First we have to get there, that is why there is a plan. We will redefine capital, we will achieve an economy based on resources. We will repair our world while stopping the wholesale rape of it's resources. We will clean the planet of all of it's trash, the plastic in it's oceans, the bags littering the land. We will make a new beginning for ourselves and our children. If you agree with even a small part of what I have outlined here, then read forward and give it a thought.

Imagine our world without "nation states," where would we find our conflicts? The people of Iran actually like Americans. Americans do not want the people of Iran to suffer due to their leaders actions. However, America has not only pushed for sanctions, they are proud of their ability to enforce those sanctions. That is the pride of the Nation State. Not to mention the pride of the American Empire. Politicians figured out long ago that men will fight for a flag when they will not fight for a particular agenda. Hide the agenda behind a flag and men will kill without caring why. National pride is a form of bait and switch. I would never say that I am not proud to be an American (because I am) but that doesn't mean that I agree with all of our policies. However, if I say, "We can't do that to those people!" All anyone has to do is question my patriotism. That is why the Nation State has to go, if we are going to fight one another in the future let's do so for a reason not for a cloth. Oh, I did say that there is an American Empire, if you cannot see it, then you are blind to the world. (I actually had an American Veteran tell me that there was no empire! Really? What planet are you living on?)

How do we accomplish this? Each and every human on the planet is born into a family! Sounds obvious, what does it have to do with politics? Everything! New political system to be born on the back of the family by creating a "Chain of Councils." Every family to have a council which decides how they will live as a family. That is not to say that we will actually allow our children a voice in how they are raised, it is merely a starting point for a true democracy.

Each Family Council will have a representative in it's community. Each Community Council to have a representative in it's District Council, and they will have a representative in it's city council. Each City Council to have a representative in it's district council. Each District Council to have a representative in it's city council. Each City Council to have a representative in it county council. Each County Council to have a representative in it's state council. Each State Council to have a representative in it's national council. Each National Council to have a representative in the World Council. All politics is local. Families will develop their district, their city, their county, their state, their nation and their world in a way that serves them best. Laws and rules will be handled on the council level in which it effects. This is an outline, the people of the world will have to decide how best to deal with the bureaucracy created by such a system. It will surely be better than the one we have now. One Family World rule.

Sounds simple enough to begin with, but there are companies, corporations, nations, peoples and special interests who will do ANYTHING to prevent this from happening. But they cannot stop it, it started the second I started writing. How could we possible "elect" these representatives without once again skewing the system to special interests? Easy, every radio station, television station in the world will GIVE so much time to candidates in prime viewing/listening times based on level of office. They will do this or they will lose their broadcast licenses. Each candidate would also receive an equal amount of resources in order to run a level and fair campaign. Oh, did I mention that each and every person would be REQUIRED to vote. This will create a true democracy based on community, that will be ruled equally, with the people determining their own fate.

What do we do about lobbyists and special interests? We make lobbying outside of the council system illegal. Politicians, once elected would be fitted with a device similar to google glass which will record, for posterity (and our personal freedoms), all conversations and meetings held in (or out) of office. If you want the job, take the leash!!! All representatives will be bound by the laws exactly, in every method and way, as they are applied to the general populace. Each politicians DS ("digital self", we will expand on this later) will be recorded and "broadcast" 24/7. No back room or bathroom deals. No exploitation of any people or resources for the benefit of a few!

Boy, you are a dreamer! How could we keep our economy going in such a utopian system? Simple, simple, simple! Society has been bumping around the edges of it's own answers without seeing it. We turn our capitalist system on it's head from exploitation of resources to the ECONOMY of resources. We throw away all of our "currencies" and develop an new currency based on equity of resources. Much the same way as "Bitcoin" works, without BITCOIN of course. You equalize what resources are worth based on other resources with each system back checking every other system to prevent manipulation. (By system, I am implying that every community on the planet have it's own computer/server system that tracks it's resources along with the resources of every other community. It may be that we will have to tier this system so that the communities of one state back check those in the same state, etc.)

We now have the capability to keep track of the resources of the world and to balance those resources worldwide. Resources belong to all of the people of the world. (I don't think that can be said enough, otherwise someone out there will decide that a particular group of resources or products belongs to them alone.) Intellectual properties will also belong to the people, we will have to have an "open-source" information system in order to advance our race at the pace required to sustain it.

Manufacturing will occur locally for all products. We can build manufacturing facilities that can supply ANY good you require on demand. Besides spending your resources for the goods themselves, you will purchase the "idea/design/blueprint" for a product. This is a trend anyone can see coming, it will be much the same as buying a book on Amazon and having it immediately downloaded. Since we have "open-sourced" all of the worlds information there will still be a need to reward the innovators. Because we want to encourage innovation, someone who "creates or innovates" a product or service will receive a reward relative to the size of the achievement.

We have given everyone on the planet a proud home with plenty of food on the table. (We actually haven't given anyone anything other than what they were born to.) What will drive anyone on the planet to work in this system? Back to family. Everyone on the planet will be educated and assessed to put their particular skills to work. Everyone will be required to work according to their capacity to do so. People will work for the good of their families and their communities. However, to insure this, we go back to the Bible. "A man who shall not work, shall not eat!" Now if a person is incapable of physical labor, we will find them something to do with their mind.

There is a place for everyone in the new world. Every person on the planet capable of working will work forty hours a week for nine months of the year. In return, every person on the planet will receive three hundred and twenty resource credits per week, every week of the year. This includes those who are incapable of working along with every child, every senior, every invalid, everyone. These resource credits will not be needed to feed or house you or your family. Resource credits will be used for clothing, services and merchandise that people want. Needs are rights, right?

If we apply our technology correctly it will come to pass that the most work anyone has to do is to oversee a machine that does our farming. We will surely attempt to remove as much labor from mankind's life as possible, but in doing so we have to replace that labor with creativity. Which means that mankind will always have something to do to occupy his/her time. There will be the exceptions for those who are incapable of doing anything and we will take care of them to the best of our ability. Need I say more?

Converting the cities of the world from sprawling cesspools into clean productive "hives" will necessitate a learning curve. People will go from working year around to working only nine months of a year. Working in a grocery store to working in the sustainable community gardens. No one will be useless or unemployable, we will back away from using huge tractors to farm huge tracts of land to sustainable farms where people do the work cleanly and efficiently. Every person on the planet will know where their food comes from, they will have a vested interest in the supply. The world we live in now has allowable limits of bug parts in our foods. We have allowances because we cannot be bothered to limit production to a level where our food can be kept clean. Do we want to continue that practice?

Are you telling me that we throw away our technology and go back to an agrarian society? No, I am saying we embrace our technology while at the same time eliminating "dirty" technology. Currently every calorie of food eaten requires the expenditure of seven calories of oil for it's creation. We don't have to do that anymore, we no longer need petrochemical fertilizers, by building mega-farms capable of supporting a local population, we can control everything from water, sunlight, soil conditions etc. We can control pests by instituting compartmentalization and quarantine. All excess materials created by the "hive" will be recycled. This means your leftovers and "wet" garbage will be treated, composted and rendered inert (based on the actual supply of waste) and then used for new soils. "Farms" will be bio-diverse. I could say more, but the technicians and "bio-diverse farmers" know way more than I do concerning this subject.

How? We change the way our cities are built and lived in. Imagine this city… Lying along a set of rolling hills there are thousands upon thousands of hexagonal cells protruding from their south-eastern and north-western sides. Sitting among these massive "combs" are religious centers. Threaded through the "religious" center, exists a school and beside the school is a modern library where anyone can go in and research anything, from farming organic tulips to how to build an atomic clock using a smoke detector. Not just research it, but build it. (Remember, you have a resource allocation, if you want to speed up the North Coast Highway doing 250 mph, then you can do that as long as you have the resource credits to burn) With world wide mass transit, you can go anywhere you want in the world just by getting in a pod. Around the "combs" there is a tower twenty stories tall with a footprint as large as three stadiums. It's a "farm". (more on mass transit later)

Keep in mind that we are building structures that must last at least a thousand years, so you want it EXTREMELY well built. Yes, everything we build should have a minimum life span so that not only does it pay for itself a hundred times over, but it shouldn't cost a small fortune to maintain it. Depending on where each "comb" is located, the uses for these super-farms will vary. For example, I think the first "combs" should be built in the West Bank area of Israel. (I will explain why I think that later.) On top of the building is a four million square foot "pool" which would mimic an estuary. Working in reverse this particular installation would naturally convert seawater into clean drinking water. During this process, you use those waters to feed "natural" ecosystems to support a broad range of farmed seafood. At the start of the system you can raise fish, crabs, crayfish and seaweed. The next step in the process you can raise intermediate crops that can tolerate high levels of salt. Then you raise rice in the next "natural" environment, so on and so forth until you have clean food and water all for the price of one. I digress and bow to those who know more than I about such things, my point is that we do not have to depend on profit based corporations for "fake" food anymore. Yes, you will still be able to get your McDonald's french fries. It will just be in a different world.

In conjunction with 99% of all foodstuffs produced/processed and manufactured on a local level, you use a selected area of land for free range ranching of cattle, sheep, goats, turkeys, hogs, chickens, ducks and any other domestic food source that a society/district desires. Food sources would be raised in it's most efficient form in it's selected environment. You wouldn't try and farm apples in Cuba, right? For crops/foodstuffs that are local to areas by source, they would be sourced to the rest of the world's populations as needed/wanted. All districts/states etc. would seek to achieve a resource neutral or negative state.

In the center of this "hive" there will be a multipurpose manufacturing facility. A centralized warehouse and distribution system (for food stuffs and the few imported items) along with the supplies necessary for the manufacturing facility. The only need besides those listed already is a hub for the mass transit system along with a server farm for the DS, "digital selves" of the population. I have to say that every sidewalk, every entry, every room in the city and surrounding area would be recorded. Now there would be a privacy block with a series of "forgetting" systems to delete unnecessary content. Content would only be "seen" when a crime is committed, which will happen, but there will be far fewer instances of crime in this system.

In our new one family world everyone will have the same amount of credits to spend with the exception of those whose contribution creates more wealth. How could you possible gain in such a system? By conserving resources to gain. If resources are wealth, then the conservation of resources is the only way to create new wealth! If you worked for an entity who developed phones for example, and you figure out a way to increase its durability so that it lasts ten years instead of five, then you have created wealth by reducing the amount of resources needed by society. By creating this wealth, you will receive the adulation of society along with a one time reward directly related to the amount of resources conserved.

The point in not allowing long term dividends from creating wealth is that it would create an oligarchy once again.

This is the system that we are fighting to shake off now. This is also why there will be resource caps on the amount that any one individual can spend in any given year. It will also necessitate an estate tax of eighty percent of resource credits saved. Anyone will be able to develop their own projects/hobbies or self educate in order to change their skills along with the method in which they contribute. Anyone can create new items for "consumption" by the masses, however, creating a product will inherently reduce the amount of resources available hence a resource cap on frivolous spending. (More on the bases of resource credits later)

I have to add one thing here, I am spit balling. Just because I have laid out a direction doesn't mean that the people have to accept it whole. There are billions of people and all of them have their own opinions. I am making suggestions based on what I believe is best for us and the planet. It will ultimately depend on each community to decide how best to achieve our goals.

Chapter 3 Economy and Resources

So we base our new economy on "ECONOMY". To call what we have today an "economy" is a joke. We also base it on the ecology. We undertake projects all over the world to clean up the world. We remove the plastic from the oceans, the trash from the lands, re-naturalize the world in order to meet TRUE balance with nature and our needs. We tear up the interstates and roads that clutter up and divide our planet, we develop raised platform mass transportation. Our countries have based their economies on hundred year old technology with the automobile, it is wholly unnecessary. That doesn't mean that if we couldn't leave a few roads for posterity, along with a few automobiles for use on vacations etc.

Can you imagine, how will people get to their homes if you tear up the roads? Well, here's the thing, people who live in homes outside of new concentrated cities (we'll talk more about that later) can stay in their homes for the remainder of their lives, however, as these generations die off, their properties will be converted back into a natural state or used for farming as the need for resources is balanced. If someone chooses to stay in their existing home, they will be charged a "resource" tax. Their refusal to concentrate requires us to leave a road, tolerate their auto's and keeps us from letting nature reclaim their property. Not a cheap proposal by any means.

Concentrating the populations of the world to areas where people want to live and where their families have traditionally lived, we can streamline transportation costs, food costs and end urban sprawl all in one fell swoop. As properties are dismantled for conversion back to a natural state, all of the resources from that property will be recycled. The only concession to that is our ability to laser scan the "old" world and recreate it in one of our "digital universes". (More on that later.)

Conservation of resources can be reduced by recycling, but to get to a point where there are enough resources for everyone is to build for time. If you purchase a new electronic item, it should be a viable for the next ten years instead of ten months. A washer, dryer, dishwasher, hot water heater, stove, refrigerator, microwave, garbage disposal and any other product created using extremely modified resources should be built to last at least fifty years with each and every piece to be recycled at the end of it's life-cycle. Everything we make should be sustainable, non-toxic, recyclable and it should increase the quality of life for all. At the same time we will mine our old landfills for the resources that we buried out of ignorance.

We have a great representation system and we have an economy based on economy. I realize you can see a thousand problems with no answers, I see nothing but solutions. What would we use for "currency"? Well, in an economy based on economy, you would be allocated a set amount of resources that you can spend in any manner you see fit. We will have no electric bill, no water bill, no property taxes, no cable or phone bills. All of that would be provided with your home to be used for the benefit of your family. If you wanted extras, you would spend your excess resource "credits" however you want. Everyone will work in some capacity based on knowledge and ability for nine months (40 hours a week) out of the year. You will also be eligible for yearly local (to your continent) vacations with one trip anywhere in the world once every five years. (Could not be traded.)

Resources- The current economies of the world are based on fiat currencies. The problem with fiat currency is the fact that inflation is inevitable (it's built in), causing said currencies to devalue to the point that it consumes itself by being worth less than itself! What? Look at the American dollar that is worth a negative 14 trillion! That is as much as the entire world's economy for a year (if you don't count the two to four trillion in illegal/unreported and untaxed economic activity.) We have "currencies" all over the world that are worthless. To fix that problem we have to redefine capital. Is capital ink on paper? Is capital debt? Is capital a series of digital ones and zeros in a server somewhere? No. Seems to me that capital at this point is an illusion, until now. We are going to turn back the clock and make capital what it was long before modern economic theory!

Capital is only created by human thought combined with human effort to modify or produce resources. Period. There are currently about seven billion people on the planet, if everyone contributed 40 hours a week for nine months, the whole of human capital available is equal to 10,920,000,000,000,000 man hours (give or take a hundred billion or so, I am not a scientist, nor a mathematician) which if only valued at one dollar per hour would by 780 times larger than the economy of the world for an entire year.

To quantify a single resource point to use as a base for our new economy, you have to equalize the value between "human capital" and existing resources. To do this, you have to do it in the context that after a decade or two of unprecedented production, (building our new cities and infrastructure while dismantling our old world) economic growth will contract allowing mankind to work toward always improving itself while reducing the amount of resources required for a happy and productive life. With that being said, once every family has a home and a reason to produce/innovate, we still have to decide upon a value to use as a base.

Using the American Dollar as a starting point, and considering that the values of all currencies will be fixed as of the date of the singularity (November 26th 2013 at 6:00 pm central standard time). Let's say that Gold, having it's uses in electronics etc. is extremely overvalued (with current value based entirely on sentiment, even considering its scarcity) and that it's true value is a "trading" value of $21.71 per gram (about $600.00 per ounce) and let's say that a man's labor is worth two grams of gold for eight hours of labor. Going with that same train of thought, lets say that Silver is also overvalued and that it will now "trade" at $10.85 per ounce, which would equate to eight hours of labor equaling four ounces of silver.

Then you have to relate resources to foodstuffs and labor. To do this, consider that last year the world produced 723 metric tons of wheat, that's 209 pounds for every human on the planet. At today's value (day of writing) wheat is $8.20 per bushel, that's .136 cents per pound. With that being said, if you divide a mans (or woman's) workday by seven and a half minute sections, you get 64 resource credits, which is the same as two grams of gold, four ounces of silver and three hundred seventeen pounds of wheat. To crudely relate to America's fiat currency, One Resource Credit is about 0.67

cents.

Just to make all things equal, until we stabilize our new resource credits with the world's currencies, all goods will be priced at half of their listed price as of November 26, 2013. Keeping with that, to keep from destroying our companies and corporations until we can "worldize" them, all wages will be set at one half of wages as of November 26, 2013. The faster we can implement our "One Family World" the quicker we can normalize the world. Once we are able to start implementing the system, goods and services (other than those listed as "rights") will be based on actual resources plus resource credits to produce. This will reduce the costs of goods and services so drastically that they will almost seem to be free. Although, they won't be.

WHOA!!! What the "add favorite expletive here"!!! So you're saying that my labor is only worth $5.36 per hour? OK. say you currently bring home $18.00 or $8.00 per hour. Where does that money go? 20% to 30% goes to taxes right off the top. Proportional to that, another 30% to 50% goes to hidden taxes! Whatever do you mean by hidden taxes? Take a one and a half pound loaf of bread for example (takes one pound of wheat at .136 cents a pound plus half of one resource credit to produce.) Now, why does that loaf of bread cost two dollars? Greed? Partly, but at today's price, they are charging you for the resource plus a half a man hour.

Why? The loaf of bread costs two bucks, because every step of the process is taxed along the way. From the fuel in the tractor, the income tax of the tractor driver, the tax on the tractor, the real estate taxes, the taxes on the irrigation equipment, the taxes on the truck that harvests, the taxes on the truck driver, taxes on the guy who unloads the truck, taxes on the guy who feeds the wheat into the machines to thresh it, the taxes on the baker, taxes on the building the baker uses, taxes on the electricity, taxes on the phone, the internet, the computer etc, etc, etc.

I believe one of our schools of higher learning offered a ten thousand dollar prize to the economist who could figure out the amount of tax actually paid on a loaf of bread. As you can see, it's taxed at every stage of it's production. In a resource based economy, that same loaf of bread could be produced and delivered for about a third of a resource credit (or twenty cents). From here on I will refer to prices in Resource Credits rather than dollars.

You can pursue any hobby you like, if that hobby turns into a project, that turns into a company and creates a product that other people value, then you have that right. Of course the "company" will theoretically be part of the state. There will be a profit cap with everything above a certain line will go back into the resource pool. Of course in order to spur innovation and creativity, we will be able to generate a larger resource pool. However, we would all have resource caps (total amount of resources that anyone person/intimate family could use) that we could not exceed. In other words, just because you can afford to purchase a stadium full of fuel oil, that doesn't mean you could buy it. There are too many variations of rules and possibilities to contemplate for me to even get close to the system that will actually be put into place. Once again, this is merely a guideline.

Eventually, we will fully automate every job that man currently has to do. That point is coming much faster than you think. At this point, it's all about reducing the amount of resources needed. In order to do this, we limit each couple to one child. I can honestly say that this is one item that communist China got correct. Although they have recently let up on this rule because their "cheap" labor pool was starting to age. We enforce this rule worldwide…. It might take a century or two to balance our population with our limited resources, but what makes one family more important than any other? If you want to raise more than one child, you can raise an orphan as there will always be children who are not wanted by their family. Just how would I enforce this rule? Personally (and I did say personally) I would require sterilization of the couple upon the successful delivery of a healthy child.

I don't think I have to draw out every line for you to see the overall plan. So far I have only talked about the political and economic sides of this vision. Which, if you know anything about history, you know that without economic forces, you cannot change the political forces. How can we possibly manage to achieve either of these? Don't take NO for an answer. We demand these changes of our respective governments. Any country that claims to be free, cannot deny you these changes. I have always said that American's will never revolt because, "Even the poorest of the poor are well fed and entertained!" This is a revolution of the single individual claiming their own rights. How can that be wrong? I realize that I am advocating the dissolution of every government on the planet. I am also advocating the creation of a one world government. Scary stuff. It doesn't have to be. Honestly, if we are going to survive as a race, this is our only option. Unless of course you know of some way to force each existing government of complying with every other government. I know, funny isn't it? Anyway, I still have a lot to tell you. Once again, where do I go from here?

Chapter 4 Transition

Sounds good? Or a nightmare? Read on and decide. How do we transition from our rape the world capitalist society to a save the world resource society? I could say, just do it, but that would be too simple, wouldn't it? We use our existing resources to fund the transition. Keep in mind that we have wiped away all debt, hence no cash. That's OK, we have resource credits now that are actually based on something real and tangible. We leave our multinational corporations in place (structure, personnel and infrastructure, with a definite change in management, unless they are indoctrinated of course) to find, manage and reduce resource requirements. We also merge all corporations under one umbrella, the peoples umbrella. (i.e. worldize them)

Consider the requirements to build and house seven billion people. If you start with the premise that the average family has seven people, (which could live together comfortably with an allotment of 400 sq ft per person) then we have to build one billion homes. Of course we will need more but a billion is a good start, more than likely we will need close to two billion homes. (At two billion homes, the square footage requirements won't be as high.) Going with our theme of reducing resource requirements, let's set a target of each home lasting for a thousand years. Sounds unlikely?

So! The Romans built many things two millennia ago that stand today. The "consumer" human builds for today, not tomorrow. Older people always buy the twenty year shingles because the roof won't be their problem in twenty years. Really? We are cheap with cash and extravagant with resources. If you look back at the buildings built before the modern world, they were built to last. Granted those buildings were cathedrals, castles and other institutional buildings, but they were built to last. Today even the most important of buildings will be lucky to last fifty years. The world and everything in it is already on its head, we have to turn it back over.

Back to the impossibility of building a billion plus homes. Consider this, over the last two years, the world has produced 172 million automobiles (hundred and twenty five year old technology). If we were building homes "cells" (not prison cells, 30' hexagon homes x 50' deep) at the same production rate (not only can we meet that level of production, we can exceed that rate by two fold) every family on the planet will have a sustainable home within a decade. Within another decade, every couple and small family could have their own home. Twenty years of resource heavy production along with the greatest period of innovation in history will allow us to achieve the goal of being resource neutral.

Where do we get the materials? Currently there are 1714.28 pounds of plastic for every person on the planet. Plastic from petrochemicals will be limited in production and only used where no other product will work. Had to get that in there. Back to what I was saying, at 1714.28 pounds of plastic per person, that gives a family of seven people a wonderful twelve thousand pounds of plastic to work with. We convert this plastic into a binder, mix it with recycled asphalt to produce a pourable cement like product. With this product we extrude large half hexagon cells that can be stacked into homes. Then we line them with a layer of "air" as an insulator (which will also act as a route for electrical and plumbing systems) and then coat the inside with a layer of shot-crete. Then the inside of these "cells" could be decorated however a family desired. Yes, each home will be finished. Each of these "cells" will be able to be stacked to create HUGE complexes. Between each of these cells is a four foot layer of earth.

Once again, this is merely one possibility. We have tens of thousands of tons of resources buried in landfills all over the planet. I have heard of a technology that allows all trash to be flash steamed into an inert material. This inert material (with a large plastic content) can be formed into any shape. It can be extruded, pressed, poured etc. to create an infinite amount of shapes for building. There is no reason that it cannot be extruded directly into a hexagon shape and stacked for housing. The reason I chose the hexagon shape is nature. If it works for bees, it will work for us. The top and bottom angles of the hexagon can be equivalent to a four/twelve pitch on a home with the "floor" accessible for those ever necessary utility systems.

Back to back we place them so one faces south-east and

the other faces north-west. The front of your home (the only side exposed to the outside) will have "smart" glass at the bottom that will allow light in to moderate the temperature. The top twenty-two feet of the "glass" in front will be highly efficient solar cells to power all of your low power devices. All your electronics, your televisions, anything that can be run on low voltage DC will be. We will actually build "mountains" of humanity. The concentration of resources combined with a concentration of manufacturing and distribution gives us economies of scale never dreamed of before. It's almost too much to take in. But there is more, much more.

Consider the water supply to this "mountain" of "cells". Each gallon will be used to it's optimum. Fresh treated water will be supplied for drinking and cooking. Water from catch basins (rain water) will be lightly treated and then used for showers, watering plants, washing dishes and clothes. That water will drain away and be lightly treated then returned for use in flushing toilets. Once it has been used in the waste stream the water is treated and then returned into the natural environment. Yes, we will figure out a way to get our drugs and vitamins etc. out of the water so we don't have fish on steroids. (Graphene filters is one thought, water vapor will go through, but not much else will.) Leveraged use of water decreases the need for so much fresh water (which you will not have to pay for, but there will be limits, you cannot fill your neighbors "basement" with water and go swimming). Also consider that we will use macro-generation to get every ounce of electricity out of every movement. When you flush, a series of small generators will be turned creating very small amounts of juice, however when you multiply that by ten thousand flushes every few hours, there is real potential there.

Using the bathroom! Smart toilets will know what you're doing and divert that waste appropriately. Urine will be recycled for its phosphates to use as fertilizer as well as converted to hydrogen. Every spare volt will be used to make hydrogen as it is the most efficient way to store energy. The entire complex will be energy efficient and an energy producer. It's goal will be to become energy neutral where it requires no outside electrical system. Here's the thing, very few of these ideas are original.

I titled this chapter transition. How do we prove it works and where do we start? How about Palestine? Every year we send billions in aid to Israel and hundreds of millions to the Palestinians. We take those same funds and we build three hundred thousand homes in sustainable cities for the Palestinians. Along with the homes we build modern infrastructure for fast reliable mass transit, a bio diverse food farm and a manufacturing and distribution center. We cannot forget to add a school or two to the mix. We won't spend a penny more than we normally do in a year and it might take a year or two to get it going, but we can end the conflict in Israel tomorrow.

The biggest problem the Palestinians have with the Israelis is the expansion of housing complexes in the West Bank. Every time Israel says, "We are going to build 2500 homes!" the Palestinians feel that they are being put upon. Israel wasn't an empty land when the Jewish people returned. Extend an olive branch, build sustainable communities for the Palestinians that they can be proud of. Of course, the Palestinians will do the actual building. This will provide them good jobs with good income until our new system is fully in place.

Imagine if Israel announced today that they were going to use the aid from the U.S. for building communities for the Palestinians. Provided the Palestinians used their aid for the same use. What would be left for them to fight over? There is plenty of land for both "states." Although our system does away with states, borders and petty bureaucrats! If everyone in the land of Israel had a productive, successful and happy home, why would they throw rocks? Palestinian men (16 to 30) have NOTHING to do but fume and plot the downfall of Israel. Wouldn't it be wise to get them on your side? Especially considering that you have to live with these people as neighbors.

Palestine is where you start, then you move on to Haiti, the Philippines, Afghanistan, Iraq and then Detroit. Yes, where we need it most and where it can do the most good. It will work, we just have to start. In the Philippines for example, we build our "human" mountains of cells, but the lower cells will be concrete reinforced between the cells and the rear of each cell will have "blow out points" so that a huge wave doesn't come along and push the whole "mountain" into the sea. These lower levels will be dedicated to manufacturing or some other use, it would be foolish to put peoples homes in the direct path of destruction.

Of course that's a job for a senior engineer, isn't it? But we can build LONG term housing that can withstand everything with the exception of a ten-thousand year storm. By design, these "mountains" should hold up very well in an earthquake as they are only connected by flexible plumbing systems and are separated by three to four feet of earth, depending on the amount available near the site.

In our homes, we use as much natural light as possible, then as a backup we use materials that store light and emit if back in the evening. We will mine our existing landfills and reuse/re-purpose/recycle every resource there. We will reduce or eliminate the need for "new" resources (such as coal, which we won't need) Everything will be recycled or reused to get the most value out of every resource. Severely limit the use of fossil fuels. We will have very little use for oil. However, we will maintain a plethora of vehicles to be used for vacations, or for straying off grid, or a Sunday drive permitted you have the resource credits to do so. Which you should because there will be no house payment, no rent, no electric bill, no taxes, no water bill, no land tax, no car payment (if you want to use a car, you just use one of the many belonging to you and your community), no grocery bill, oh my! What am I to do with my "credits" Use them to drive across America on it's one last remaining interstates. Sounds fun, huh?

We start to seriously "Engineer" our planet! We have been doing so for the last two centuries without realizing it, and not to our benefit. We can reverse global warming, we can reduce carbon dioxide levels to per-industrial levels in a decade or less. We can cool the oceans in front of a hurricane and take away it's brute force. We could actually cool the ocean enough to stop a hurricane or a typhoon in its tracks. All it takes is an idea, a little engineering, and the will to do it. Why not? We could actually screen off part of the sun that hits the planet and cool it. We can also find out what the hell they use that harp thing for and decide if it's good for us or not. They are probably talking to "people" in another dimension and every time they communicate, it causes a rift in the planet (would explain the earthquakes and volcanoes that have "woke" up recently!)

OK, talking to another dimension? Probably not, heating up the ionosphere so that there is a drought in Russia, probably so. Who knows? That will be one great thing about "open sourcing" all information on the planet, we get to learn all of the dirty little secrets. However, we have to agree as a people that those things happened in the "old" world and that we cannot carry any animosity or anger toward another group for what was done in an upside down world. The world we live in now is the upside down world, to turn it over will be extremely painful. It must be done. What must be kept in mind though is forgiveness. If we carry any animosity forward for how a people or a government acted in this strange environment, then we will never be able to move on.

Speaking of "open sourcing" all information, I cannot even imagine how innovative the world will become once all information is known. Just think about the five largest computer software companies and how far our technology could/will advance once their proprietary information is known. There is one consideration however and that is the information that must be kept secret in order to keep our information secret. Now if that doesn't give you a headache, I don't know what will. The "chain of councils" will have the ultimate say on that. Period

Chapter 5 What do we gain?

That's always the defining question when humans are involved. It's a lot like having a wife, "what have you done for me lately?" Once our plan is in place the worlds population will stabilize and then slowly it will reduce itself into a manageable number. Personally, I would say about three billion is about right. It would actually be better with less, but I am not into genocide. What will be the deciding factor in the final population size will be what size population can live comfortably with a pre-determined allowance of resources. What I mean by this is that seven billion people will ultimately consume say one and a quarter earths worth of resources in a year. We have to reduce that to a sustainable number. It may be that two billion people require one quarter of what the earth can produce/provide in a year.

I would say that is safe number because it will allow us a four to one margin of safety in case of a disaster of some sort. If you're right there on the edge pushing population with resources as we do today, all it takes is one large drought or whatever to cause mass starvation. Isn't it better to limit population rather than risk death on a massive scale? Within twenty years through the leveraging of our technology and our resources, we will have the highest quality of life while using the minimum amount of resources possible. I don't know what that magic number will be, it might be seven billion, although I highly doubt it, I just can't say. What I do know is that if we continue with the systems we have now, we are all doomed.

The largest gain in resource management will come from not having to continually replace existing resources. If you buy a washing machine made today, it is made using the minimum amount of resources required, but it's lifespan is limited to about five years. That's B.S. With stable homes, reliable mass transit (that we will love) and a sustainable, clean and unadulterated food source, we will have an excess of human capital available to do the truly important work of mankind. (I will go into that more later) With no house payment, water bill, electric bill etc, those 8 resource credits per hour looks pretty good, doesn't it? You can no longer look at those 8 resource credits as $5.36 per hour, you have to see it for what it really is, human capital.

OK. one hour of work is worth 8 resource credits, no matter if I am a rocket scientist or a janitor, right? Not exactly, we need a basis for trade. Think of the 8 credits as sort of a minimum wage. Just like our "old" world, you can leverage your worth via education and innovation. By giving everything on the planet an equalizing value, resources, man hours etc, you create real wealth. Each person, family, community, district, city, county, state, country and nation will place it's value and it's wealth into the amount of resources conserved, instead of on valueless debt of other nations. What? No more banks to devalue our labor, our money and our lives? Right, no more banks. Banks will no longer be able to devalue a man's contribution to his family, community etc. The only way to create wealth in our new world is to create resources and then conserve those same resources. Consider this, isn't there greater value in the Amazon basin as a jungle than there is in the value of the trees themselves? By building our one point eight billion homes, we reduce the need for those trees as resources. The only trees we will need from now on will be those that are farmed specifically for their use as wood and pulp. (we will find a way to recycle paper more than a couple of times, there has to be a way to rebuild those fibers so they can be used again, and again, and again, it's all about our tech now).

How is that all possible? Design, technology and innovation. I can have a preliminary blueprint of sustainable long term (thousand years at least) housing (or home or cell, whatever you prefer) in a few days that could be stacked to make our "mountains of humanity" and could be built for twelve thousand resource credits per unit! Why? Because we have this ONE chance in history to change, and there is no other way to do it and do it humanely. If we stay on the current path, the worlds resources will continue to be drained at a rate of one and a half earths per year…. unacceptable. At the current rate of consumption, nation will be at war with nation until we are all destroyed by our own greed. The communists once said that they would hang us with the rope that we sold them. What they didn't realize was that the noose is for them as well.

Scary huh? We all change or we all die, no other choice.

Want to know what the intelligentsia of the world have decided is the best answer to our current decline? They plan to kill off 99% of the worlds population. No? Why? Yes, with one percent of the worlds population remaining (only the really rich or the really useful will be spared) they can continue to rape our planet while squandering it's wealth on useless toasts to another yacht on a sea of blood. Here's the thing, if the people of the world decide that they want to create our one family world, then those who control the world today will rise up and give us a war like you have never seen. They will not let go of the levers of power without a struggle. Their families have worked for generations to solidify their wealth and power. No they will not let go easily. To get our "perfect" world, we will have to wade through rivers of blood.

If we don't change the world today and take those levers of power out of their hands, then there will be oceans of blood. I will probably say that again, and again. You have to understand that in order to change the world you have to take a stand and NOT BACK DOWN. If we take one step back, they will push us three more steps back. It is us who will do the real pushing, it's us who control the real wealth of the world and it is us who WILL change it. When I say we already control the worlds wealth, I am not talking about gold or any other tangible asset. I am talking about the worlds labor, not one more dime can be produced unless we produce it. Their food comes out of the same fields as ours does. They have their means, we have ours. That is not to say that it will be easy, because it wont. They control the military's of the world, luckily most of the people who make up those military's come from "poor" families. The people who they will make war against are the fathers, brothers and sons of the warriors.

I remember watching the news during the March on Wall Street. They asked those kids (and adults) what they wanted, they didn't have an answer. I started to wonder, what could they want? Finally the answer to it all hit me like a brick. Most of the ideas in this text belong to someone else (not all of them) but if we want to be truly free, we all have to do it together. The whole world must rise up as one and take the reins of power and give them back to the people where they belong. I digress, I get side-tracked quite easily, especially when I am passionate about something. I realize that you are still wondering why I am saying that the singularity is here. Keep reading, you will get it before we are done here.

Back to the wealthy rulers of our upside down world. We allow them to keep their Park Ave. apartments, their Rolex watches, their conspicuous limos. But we take everything else, their companies, their power, their private jets. And if they sit quietly at home and don't stir up too much trouble, we let them live…Harsh I know, I am not advocating murder. Unless they decide that murder is the only tool left to them. They might try to shut down our networks, (our weakness is their weakness) but when they do they will cripple the financial system that is the backbone of their system. I honestly believe that the system has expanded past the point of shutting it down. With the cell phone system integrated into the "net" there are just too many "nodes" for them to kill them all. That doesn't mean that we don't have our weaknesses besides that. One of our greatest weaknesses is what will eventually allow us to be free, rule by all of the people. Until we defeat them, we will have to have some form of centralized command, otherwise everyone will be fighting from their own viewpoint/angle and it will be impossible to make progress in that type of environment. There has to be some sort of fail safe. Allow one person or one committee to direct your efforts and they have to be cut loose once it's all said and done.

I want to say one more thing about the transition and not only why it has to happen, but why you should want it to. To deny your neighbor is to deny yourself. I think that says it all right there, but let me put it this way. Our current system is only capable of supporting 43% of the people on the planet, the other 57% will scrimp by on less than two dollars a day until they die of malnutrition, malaria or one of many other "poor" man's diseases. (Statistics via Buckminster Fuller) Are we barbarians? After the atrocities of World War II, our American politicians declared that we would never allow something like that to occur again. Really? Look to Darfur, we had no personal, nor more importantly, any business interests in the region, so we stood back and watched as half a million people or more were slaughtered. Really?

Really? A christian nation? No, not so much. I have tried

to keep God out of this discussion so far, but eventually we will have to deal with faith. The whole world cannot unite unless we all find common ground. There is common ground, we are all one family. We are all human and can see the need to be humanitarians. All of us. Period.

Chapter 6 Freedom

I live in the "Land of the Free" a title that we American's love to wear. But we are NOT free, we are far from it. Oh, you are free to starve here, but that's about the extent of it. Don't get me wrong, I love my country, although I believe the usefulness of the Nation State has passed. We are beyond that now as a species. I am surprised that there are still Kings and Queens in this world, their time expired a century ago. Mankind obviously had to take political missteps in order to reach the path we have before us. We had to have dictators, republics, socialist republics, communist republics, it all led us here to this point in time. We have one choice, adapt or die.

The infrastructure of our "old" world was paid for with public funds, the dams that hold back our rivers and generate our electricity were paid for by our grandfathers. Why in the name of all that's holy should I have to pay for water or electricity? Isn't housing a right? Isn't decent food (unadulterated) and clean non-toxic water a right? We have to pay for these things in order to support our burgeoning bureaucracies. Totally not necessary. We currently have entities (Highland Park Water Department, outside of Detroit) who are busy destroying their customer base in order to support a city! This city decided that it's water dept. was going to be a cash cow and save this community. In order to do this, they sent out water bills to their customers for anywhere from two to nine thousand dollars. Saying that this was due to leaks or from miss-reading the meter for years. So they have an incompetent workforce that overlooked obvious problems for years then put that burden back on the people who they exist to support! Shouldn't those people have the option of scaling back their water department instead of the water department scaling them back? And get this, the people who couldn't afford or refused to pay? They added their bill to the tax rolls so that if it isn't paid inside of two years, they can take their homes. The people should control the system, not the system controlling the people.

Our world is UPSIDE DOWN. If you cannot see that, I cannot show you. We waste resources then measure our success by the amount of wanton consumption of contrite/needless goods. 50% of the crap you have in your home is more or less useless. Most of the "stuff" that you have you wont touch for months at a time. Why have it? Because your neighbor does? 90% of the plastic crap for sell at your local retail location is useless. If as a society we decide that all of humanity has value and that value is the only source of wealth, well then we have created an economy that will dwarf the decaying corrupted system of old.

Chapter 7 Energy

Electrical energy. Mankind can hardly go forward without it. For the last century, we have powered our world with hydrocarbons. To quote a Saudi prince, "The stone age didn't end for a lack of stones!" We have squandered the hydrocarbons of our planet, what we must do from here forward is CONSERVE our oil. We must use it when its the only choice. The U.S. declares that it has become energy independent thanks to new technology. This technology has allowed it to exploit their huge natural gas fields. This will be invaluable while transitioning to a pure electrical energy system. Unfortunately this same discovery has set back "green energy" decades because there isn't one large source of pollution, the thousands of little sources fall below levels regulated by the E.P.A. Transitioning our world to a "One Family World" while changing the energy we use to pure electrical just might save us in time.

Once it's no longer needed, we can conserve our fossil fuels and not only stop global warming, but reverse it. Yes, pure clean electrical energy is not only possible it has been possible for the last seventy years. It is also possible to reverse global warming and to stabilize temperatures for the long term. Yes, people are more than capable of harnessing the energy of the earth. We are capable of manipulating the planet and it's weather for the greater good. This isn't purely theoretical, it is possible if we are willing to spend the political capital required. This is not a question of "if we can afford to" it's a question of "can we afford not to."

Where are we going to get all of the energy for our utopia? The average ocean depth is about two and three quarters of a mile deep. Imagine a structure equal in size to four football fields. This structure is part ship, part submarine and all energy. It is stabilized twenty to thirty feet below the waterline with at least two and a half miles of depth beneath it. Under it are hundreds of what look like elongated fuel tanks, each being about fifty feet tall and twenty foot around. These are suspended from their narrow ends with a hybrid steel and carbon fiber cable from beneath the "plant". Each "tank" in turn seeks to add enough water when at it's top stroke causing it to sink. Once it has sunk to the bottom of its stroke it pumps out enough water to make it rise again.

These tanks will be pressurized which will make it easier to pump out the excess water at the bottom of the stroke. To complete one cycle should take each tank three to five hours depending on the depth of ocean where the plant is located. As each tank goes through its cycle the "life line" cable is engaged via a transmission to one of the turbines inside the "plant." This allows you to gear the cycle so that you get the most power from each stroke. This also keeps the "tanks" from popping up on its upstroke which would prevent the system from utilizing all of its potential energy. That's basically all there is to it. This system isn't exactly ready for implementation, but it does use "off the shelf" technology so that very little engineering will need to be done. Because the system moves at such a "slow" speed, there is no danger to sea life.

The biggest challenge to this besides politics, is reducing power transmission losses over long distances. Something that can be worked out in no time with humanity working together toward its major goals. I understand that carbon nanotubes the potential to carry electrical energy long distances with zero losses. Why aren't we investing in these types of projects? We're not because there is just too damn much money in hydrocarbons. If people knew that we could generate all of the electricity that our civilization needs without draining the planet dry, they might just revolt.

You want to hear something really funny? I contacted green energy companies, federal energy authorities and governments all over the world trying to sell them this system. I finally decided that I had to give it to all of you. They don't want you to know that the world is one great engine and that we only have to put a wire here and a switch there in order to use it. There are other ways we can generate all of the power we need as a civilization without trashing our planet. Not only do we have to develop this system and ones like it, but we have to reduce the power we actually use. Once again by concentrating our populations, we gain huge efficiencies where power use is concerned.

If you go back to beginnings of electrical use and it's history, there was a war of sorts between two competing systems, there was Westinghouse and Tesla with alternating current against General Electric and Edison with direct current. Eventually Westinghouse won, but not because they were better advertisers (at least they didn't electrocute elephants like Edison,) they won because of the economic viability of their system. Turns out though, that both of them were right in their own way. We can use both systems in concert with one another to gain HUGE efficiencies.

We also need to develop what I call "micro-generation" using small wind turbines, solar etc. to power everything less than an appliance. Simple enough, by using small generation systems we free up more of our resource allocations for other uses. Wherever there is a stream, even if it only runs a week in a month, we have to use it. Micro-generation systems that will only produce hydrogen when working. By using these micro systems to generate hydrogen we effectively "store" that energy for later use. Those reserves build up and then we use them when needed. With enough micro-generation stations, we could reduce large scale generation by a minimum of ten percent.

What we have to realize is that we are capable of engineering our planet for our species, the largest obstacle to that is political. Every few years a hurricane (or it's twin, the typhoon) causes billions of dollars worth of damage taking untold lives along with it. The antarctic produces hundreds of millions of gallons of supercooled water, if we built a pipeline system from the antarctic to the Caribbean, we could reduce the surface temperature of the ocean when needed, which in turn would reduce or eliminate the threat to land. We could also use these temperature variations across the planet to generate even more juice to power our world. Political will is the problem, not lack of technology. I realize that the "cooling" system I just described is a huge undertaking. That doesn't mean I advocate building such a system, (as there is no calculating the ramifications of such a project) the point of describing it was to demonstrate the scope of our capabilities.

We have to keep in mind that just because we are capable of engineering our planet, that doesn't mean that we should. I can see ending or reducing large storms, I can see minimizing the danger of tornado's. I can see space elevators and immense bio diverse farming towers. I can also see large tracts of land reclaimed by nature. Picture seventy percent of the land converted to it's natural state with twenty percent used for food and resource production and ten percent used for cities and their associated infrastructure. There have to be limits, we can get into a technological free-for-all where we end up engineering a system simply because we can. We have to be vigilant or we will end up destroying the exact thing we are trying to save, ourselves.

Food will be locally sourced, as locally as possible. Every person will have a certain amount of calories allocated to them daily, how they choose to use/spend them is entirely up to them. Not just calorie based, but nutritionally based. Clean water is a given. Saturation and storage of excess carbon dioxide will become one of our first priorities. Cleaning the environment world wide will be our next priority. Each family, clan, village, city etc will be responsible for "their" lands. If your city chooses to waste it's resources and litter their space, then they should pay with resource allocation "taxes." Change to prosper. Environmental cleanup will work in a similar way. With countries cleaning up all of their toxic sites they will be rewarded with a cleaner environment and eventually the first non-toxic children to be born in a century.

Once our new energy systems are in place and our resources are accounted for, based on sustainable production, along with a 100% recycling system, products will become cheaper and cheaper (resource wise) to produce. The "cheaper" the more ubiquitous the item. Not everyone will want a Mickey Mouse watch, but those who do, will be able to acquire one. We are not taking manufacturing away, we are merely streamlining and allocating it to suit us. As a civilization, we will be able to give more time to moving our civilization forward. Without cash, without polluted politicians and competition for resources, there will be no need for war. No need for theft, no need for crime.

We have covered politics, the economy and energy. All of it is possible, yes! What about the social structure? You really can't cover social structure without discussing the cities first. I am all for concentrating the populations into idyllic cities. There will still be small towns, (as small as possible as long as it is sustainable) why would you move everyone to one place on the planet. For example, a county has one large city, two small towns and several burgs. You merely concentrate them by building small sustainable burgs by themselves or in groups according to their populations. This will allow us to convert most of the world into usable wilderness for the enjoyment of everyone. (There are small populations of native tribes around the world which should be allowed to live as they always have as long as they remain resource neutral.)

Eden is possible. Imagine if you would a beehive. Hives are divided and connected by cells. We could build prefabricated homes out of hexagonal cells. Stacking them and staggering them so each home receives eight hours of direct sunlight per day. A row of octagonal cells 30' in diameter and 50' long gives you a little over a twenty four hundred square feet on two levels, this should be enough space for a family of seven. Seven is the magic number to start, once we achieve a home for every family, then we can concentrate on providing homes for smaller family units. A row of cells can go for miles and can be set back to back and stacked as high as required to house the population of a given city. Making the structures a hundred to two hundred and fifty feet deep and up to twelve hundred feet high. (With the actual homes only being fifty feet deep, there will be "cells" set between them 'front to back' for water, fuel and hydrogen storage.) Each cell will have at least four feet of earth between it and the next one on every side. One end will be a glass/solar panel hybrid which would supplement its own heating and cooling needs. It kind of sounds boring, right? Two billion homes all built the same. What we gain is efficiency and they can be placed in an infinite combination of ways allowing each city to have a "feel" of it's own. The saving grace of this design is that there are literally billions of ways to furnish the interior.

There is no need for stores, the lowest level of cells could be used as "shopping" alternatives. You go into one of these "stores" where you can search any "store" for any product. Centralized shipping (through mass transportation systems) along with warehouse delivery of any item you require (if its made somewhere where the resources are available and to ship the resources would cost more than the product.) Can you imagine how much money is wasted every year on building, maintaining, managing and heating and cooling retail space. Retail space that we no longer need. All resources can be warehoused according to the needs of a population. As a society, capitalism (even though it paved the way for the future) includes huge wastes of economy. How many resources would you imagine are expended for one loaf of bread? If we can manufacture, distribute and warehouse thousands of products in one place rather than in thousands of competing entities, we gain huge economies of scale.

Mass transit and mass shipping of goods. (where required) At one time the U.S. had a good start on mass transit. It still survives in islands of prosperity, but it is inadequate in the best of conditions. As a nation, (speaking of the United States) we have squandered generations of wealth on the automotive. If we had spent those same funds on high-speed rails, distributed pod systems along with centralized living and distribution, the cost to go from New York to L.A would be no more than a cup of coffee. We tend to use a gallon of gas to transport one individual up to fifty miles (depending of course) whereas that same gallon of fuel could transport as many as twenty five people up to thirty miles.

Which would be a net gain of four hundred and fifty miles, equal to a 1400% increase in production from the same resource. Not to say that we should use fossil fuels, we should restrict their use. (With the exception of going for a drive up the coast in a 68' Impala with your girl. Just because we don't need the auto anymore doesn't mean that we should trash them all. We will need vacations and the ability to blow off steam.)

How do we get around? Before we concentrate the populations, there will be a need for transportation to and from the remote areas in which we currently live. Electric cars are the bridge from private to public transportation. Using your allotment of resources (and those of your combined family) you can "purchase" a car for local use. For long trips, you can use one of the many cars owned by your community (if your needs are outside of the existing mass transit system at the time.) The other option is to have "smart" transportation hubs based on the family, community and the district. Say you want to go to town to "purchase" a gift for your anniversary. You go online, click "pick up in ten" and within ten minutes, a vehicle assigned to your community/neighborhood, picks you up and takes you to your next location. If you live outside of a "hive" your first location might be another hub where you will board a train or a pod rail to take you into the "city" proper. If you're traveling to another city or country, you're taken to your "hives" central transportation terminal where once again, you switch methods of transport. This could be one of Space/X's new electric jets, or a transcontinental super-high speed rail. I can envision trains running at up to and over fifteen hundred kilometers per hour.

Chapter 8 Connectivity and Laws

This is the part that's going to freak you out. The part that nobody's going to like. Currently (I know I say that a lot) the people of the world (especially the younger generations) are tech savvy. Nearly everyone on the planet has a device to link them to the rest of the world. Now this device is typically a cellphone (hybrid, meaning it's a camera, television, a instant video messenger, texting etc). In the very near future this device will become our DS (digital self). So, we are all to submit to big brother? No! What we are doing is putting our foot down on big brothers neck by embracing and owning our DS. Our DS will be "keyed" to each individual and will record your entire life, every interaction, every minute of your life and that of every other human on the planet. If you have an interaction with another individual, there will be two "recordings" of the moment.

Now here's the foot for Big Brother, as long as no crime is committed, no one has a "right" to that record besides yourself and the person you interacted with. Say someone is murdered, their digital self will "scream" across it's connections and the guilty party will have to submit their "record" along with the victims record. There will be no denying the act. How could we possibly control this amount of information and how would you "police" it? We will get there in a minute. Yes, this is going to happen. However if we allow this to happen in our "capitalist" society, our privacy will never be our own. Even if you're the President of Germany or the Prime Minister of England, someone will read your mail and listen to your phone calls. What I am trying to say is that we can either have Big Brother our we can have "Our Family".

In our new society based on the Economy of Economy, the only crimes will be those of passion or perversion. With an "all knowing" digital consciousness the family will be the first to police it's own. They will defer to their community and the community will defer to the district so on and so forth. So the system will be based on tiers of "privacy." If you're in your home doing whatever it is you want to do, that "record" is your own. There is no need for anyone to have access to that unless you kill your wife or something. Which in that case, the system will already know that something is wrong and will alert both of your families. Your family will judge you for your crimes based on the beliefs of your community. That "punishment" will be approved or made harsher by the next level in the "Chain of Councils" simple as that.

Your family might be biased toward you, but no one will be able to deny the truth of their actions. Imagine how polite everyone will be! We will take the dog eat dog out of our society. It has no place in our new world. The fact is that everyone will be living two lives, their physical life and their digital life. Within a few months of implementation, the system will know what to look for and how/who to alert if there is danger to the physical self. You have to read on if you want to know more about our DS.

Of course our new world will be a society where we respect the privacy of the singular over the whole provided no one is harmed by the activities of the individual. Meaning that if you have a thousand resource credits and you want to lock yourself in your room for a weekend and blow it all on coke, go for it. It's your right. Yes, why make anything illegal as long as it harms no one else? By making anything illegal, you give it the power to regulate itself. It will feed off of your population under the surface and destroy it. Make everything legal, base its value on actual costs (including the cost of rehabilitation etc) and use the profit and the resource credits generated from its sale to strengthen your community instead of letting it rust out the bottom of your society. Make sense?

Back to the law, the real laws, I think the original ten commandments about covers everything, but each community will have to decide for itself. If you're being devious and plotting against another, that activity is certainly covered by those rules. Fortunately in our world where the economy is based on economy, man will no longer need to steal or organize their illegal activities. The kicker is that man will revert to it's true perversions. If you're in the company of someone with the same tendencies and you want to get freaky, more power to you. However, if you rape a woman or a child or anyone else for that matter, then you deserve nothing less than death, slow painful death. No treatment, no "oh, I had a bad childhood" liberal bullshit, death. If you kill someone else for pleasure, we retain the right to get medieval on you, then death. If you traffic in slaves, then you will forever be a slave to the community. Bound and chained and your DS will be deleted from the system. (Deleting someones DS will become a profound act)

Now that's just my personal views, each family and community can decide for themselves how to deal with the new types of crimes in our new world. Just remember that in our new world we have to be brutal until we are established. If you waver with anyone, you will endanger our Eden. What do we do with existing inmates? Violent and sexual offenders, that would depend on their crimes, wouldn't it? Does one who takes a life, deserve to keep theirs? No. Does someone who steals a soul by rape deserve to keep theirs? No. Really in our new society there is no reason to keep the rejects. OH NO, SANCTITY OF LIFE!!! I can hear the liberal bastards now. No, you respect all life and the lives of others or you don't deserve either.

I have to say this, you will think/believe that by making almost everything legal that society will decay faster. I believe that to a point, but by trusting people to do what's in their best interests, most will abide by a moral code. Also, families will have their own moral codes that they will expect their members to live up to. Why will this work? I believe that most people are judged more harshly by their families than by anyone else. With that said, there will be lines in the sand. What those are will be up to you and your community. The world has no business telling you that you cannot do this or that, with the exception of rape and murder.

There will still be those who will need to be "locked" away, what do we do with those? If we must imprison someone, do so with dignity. Bear the punishment on the guilty instead of on their family. Separate prisoners into their own self sustaining environments (similar to that of the rest of the population) and allow them to bear the responsibility of sustaining their own lives. Work in the garden, in the kitchen and anywhere else work needs to be done, including policing themselves. (of course we will make provisions to prevent them from just walking back into society) We won't need guards, prisoners are well known for establishing hierarchies and ruling themselves. Simple enough? Yes, it's a brutal system, but it's meant to be. The point of incarceration has been lost on our society, rehabilitation first and prevention second. I advocate a three strikes law of sorts as well, if you fail in society three times, why should we feed you?

On to connectivity. By creating our new DS in our new world and controlling the privacy of that self, we gain freedom. Our digital "profile" at this point is, a few emails, a few phone calls, a pair of striped socks from amazon and a bad pic on face page along with a click that indicates you like frozen pizza. This sounds innocuous, but the NSA or one of it's clones, can take that information and build a logic tree with it. They can know what your favorite peas are by researching that "discount" card you got at Save a Little. They can piece together a tree that connects you to a bombing in Spain ten years ago! How? Well, we are all connected by seven people or less, remember "Seven steps to Bacon" or whatever that stupid game was called? The point of it was that everyone on the planet is connected to everyone else by seven relationships or less. They can throw anyone of us away and leave us there to rot without any due process, and they can legitimately show some back room judge proof that you are connected to Joe Blow-em-up.

By taking control of the world, privatizing and layering that information, we become free as a race. Not one people free, all free. We are all slaves at this point. No chains nor are they feeding us, that cost too much. Ever read Animal Farm, I read it in school and my English teacher said that George Orwell wrote it about the Soviet Union. I thought, funny, sounds more like home. Point is, to control our privacy we have to control everything. Once we gain that control, the new digital self will be able to grow and expand on itself. As you grow, it grows along with you. Your DS will be tagged with your DNA using it as it's fingerprint. And yes, your DS will be tagged to your RFID chip along with eye scan and fingerprints and a voice print lock to keep anyone from hacking it. In fact, your DS will be able to defend itself and will warn you in real time if someone is attempting to jack it.

Within ten years your DS will be small enough to be implanted so that it could never be lost or hacked. I know, I said something that scared the hell out of all of you, RFID chips. They only make sense, the singularity (which is the combination of us all) will be sorting, filing, scanning and organizing so much data, that it will need a way to identify us. And no, you wont need your RFID tag to buy bread (because you wont have to buy food) or anything else needed for survival. But there is an up side, no one will be able to forge your signature or steal your "pod" or use your credit card (More of a resource card, no debt society, no usury, no loansharking.) (I would apologize to all of you vampires out there who make your living off of usury, but I am really not sorry.)

Our DS will allow us to govern ourselves more efficiently. If an issue arises that needs the communities attention, all of the facts can be before us and them and they can make a decision without driving to a meeting or waiting until the third Monday in the month. Issues can be dealt with as a group based on what council has jurisdiction. (Now I am not getting into that, to me ancient lines on the map are good enough to me, but remember, they are just lines, there are no more Nation States)

What's important to a family will be decided by the family, what's important to the community will be decided by the community, what's important to the district will be decided by the district and so on and so forth. When I talk about a family, I mean an entire family from Grandfather to grand kids, but I don't mean to say that the family can be ruled by a pure democratic process. If it were, candy would be on the dinner menu every night, wouldn't it?

I can picture asking my DS to do the research for this project while I sleep, then summarize the information into concise categories for me when I am ready to continue. Your DS will know if you like to be woken with a chipper attitude or if you want to be left alone for an hour. Our DS's will allow us to leverage our resources by a factor of ten. We will learn more in the next twenty years than we have ever learned before. Here's the beautiful part, every person who has a DS will be automatically linked to six other people at random around the world. Six people whom you will automatically receive updates on daily, who you can talk to and socialize with. Why? By doing this, we cut the rule of seven in half to three and a half. If were all connected to each other by seven people or less, then we will all be connected by three and a half people or less. If you can empathize with six other random people, then we become closer as a family. It's all about the numbers. The more people we care about, the less likely we are to want to war, to steal, to exploit our fellow man. At this point in progress we can give a message to someone and they could give it anyone on the planet in four people or less. Amazing.

If we all step into the light, there will be no dark corners for evil to hide in. There will be those who don't want to join us for fear of "the beast" or any number of other reasons. The truth is they are scared that they will be judged. But that's the whole point, who judges you the harshest? Your family of course! That's why we will be able to efficiently police our own from within. There will be no need for a police force, every community will have an "enforcer," but within a year or two, that won't even be necessary. People will be honest for fear of being deleted from the system. Oh, and any "enforcer" will be monitored whenever he/she is acting in this capacity to prevent abuse. Every human has the right to be treated like a human.

We either do it this way, which will require rivers of

blood. Or we stay on the current path and there will be oceans of blood. They will either kill us all off, or they will kill everyone off. (not that there is much difference except a few stay alive or we all die) There is no other endgame for the "capitalist" world. It can only end badly. Or we can all band together and take the world back from the rapists. We can all hide in our homes, watch the latest entertainment and the latest diversion (from what is actually happening) and wait to go out in one big blaze (and not one of glory.)

Before we go further, I want to prove to you that we are all one family. How many grandparents do you have? I mean all of them. How many grandparents do your grandparents have and their grandparents? If you do the math, there have never been enough people to produce the amount of people we have today. Unless, we all come from the same family! Do the math, then think about it. If you remember the guy who tricked the king by having him give him one grain of wheat on the first square of a chess board, and two on the next and four on the next and then eight, then sixteen, then thirty-two etc. etc. Your lineage works the same way, except there's a problem, the further you go back, the less people there were, but the more grandparents you are supposed to have. If you go back far enough, there are more grandparents than there are people on the planet at the time. Only one answer to that, overlap. My family is related to yours. I can say that with a hundred percent certainty. My point is that we are all one. We are a single entity and once we connect, we will create a true reflection of God. Yes, I said it. What else could it be. I am not saying that we can create God, I am saying that we can get a glimpse.

Now I keep pushing privacy, but there is an exception. If you represent your people in any council above the district council, your "record" will be open all the time. Everything you say, everything you do, everyone you meet will be an open book. No election will be bought, no resources will be traded for favors, no money will taint the process. We will have a pure democratic system. Singlism is about the individual, which by proxy is about the family. Anyone trying to defile our system will be deleted (not killed, unless that's how your district deals with that sort of thing, it's really up to you.)

Each council member (no matter the council) will vote the way the council that sent them wants them to. If there are issues that the lower council are not aware of, they shall be informed and consulted before the member votes on the issue. If they vote against the council that sent them to a higher council, then the lower council can impeach that member with a fifty-one percent majority. (everything has to be by majority, that's fifty one percent) That member will then be replaced through the same process that put him there in the first place, there will be no "interim" appointments.

Councils will appoint "leaders" for organizations and entities that serve the people. These appointments will be based on the qualifications of the candidate. Candidates will first be judged in a "blind" interview. Then hired in a "blind" vote so that favoritism or cronyism will not be an issue. In other words the candidates for any position will submit a resume without any defining personal information. On the lower councils (county/district and below) they will be unable to appoint positions without knowing the individuals involved, in which case, they will do their best to keep personal relationships from influencing their decisions. I continue trying to solve every issue that can/will be faced by this type of government. It is impossible, we are all human after all.

I also have to say this, I have talked a lot about the DS, and a lot about resources, but one point I have to make is this, ecology and environment are more important than all of that. It doesn't matter what system you have if the world cannot be lived in. Our people have disconnected themselves from nature and have embraced the church of plastic crap. Children (and adults) should spend so much time working in the bio diverse farming centers as well as connecting to nature at every chance. Nature still has so much to teach us and we haven't been paying attention. In nature only men and wolves make war and they both do so over resources.

We have the intelligence and the technology to eliminate that animalistic behavior from our world. That doesn't mean you cannot enjoy a war or two, you can do that in one of our digital universes. Gaming companies will no longer create three dimensional games with edges, they will create entire universes for us to play in. I digress

Chapter 9 Realities!!!

The technology exists in most parts of the world to implement this system now. Your digital self will be as much a part of you as your hand is now. It will monitor your heart rate, blood pressure, brain waves etc. It will become your second self. Everything that exists within that digital universe i(of which there will be many) will be just as real to you as reality is today. With the open sourcing of all research and technology, the makers of this world will have this done in a year or so. Believe it or not, it will happen.

Why not allow this to happen in our "free market" system? Right now the governments of the world control all information. Your digital self currently exists as your e-mails, your phone calls, your searching and buying habits and for many your "social" status within a "confined" community. Face-page will become world book (all internet entities will become one giant open sourced conglomerate,) everyone on the planet will exist in physical and digital reality. Now if the NSA decides that they want to know about you and your friends, they just analyze you and your friends digital selves and profile you, without your consent.

In our new world, privacy will be based on a "tier" system. No one will be able to look in on your DS without you knowing and approving of that "look". And then they will only be able to see what you want them to. If you commit a crime, then your FAMILY will have the right to look into your "digital" self and the activities that led to said crime. If your family decides that you are guilty and approves a punishment, then no problem (as long as its just) and has the approval of the next level in the "Chain of Councils". If you're found "not guilty" then the next level in the "Chain of Councils" will review and make a decision. If they find you guilty (because family can be biased) then that's that. You of course can appeal to the next level in the "Chain of Councils" but really, you're done. You will submit to the punishment deemed appropriate by your own community. Period.

I keep dancing around the subject of the new world and your DS versus the current world with your DS. What I am getting at is this, we can either take control of the system now before it's implemented (and it will be) or we can submit to the governments who control us now. Big Brother or Our Family, it's a choice that we all have to make. Take control on a local level or not. The system I am envisioning, will have a "forget" setting in it so that as so much information is created, what is irrelevant will be deleted after an appropriate period, say seven years. However, your personal DS will remember everything you have ever done. That doesn't mean your DS will punish or shame you, no, it is you. I know, hard to wrap your head around, but it's coming. We have to decide now who is going to control all of that information, us or them.

Right now we are all "slaves" to a bunch of valueless currencies in an attempt to gather tangible resources that are inherently designed to wear out and/or fail. It is designed that way so that we have to work hard constantly in order to keep current. Whatever that means. That is not an economy, that's a waste basket. Our civilization has reached it's pinnacle, it cannot grow unless we unite. And by growing I mean contracting. I can hear the Economists scream, "What about our money?" By redefining capital and exalting conservation, we will create a world economy that will shame the best days of wall street. It will be HUGE. Imagine a family whose entire capital (resource credits) is disposable. They don't have to worry about food, shelter, electricity, water, taxes etc. They can spend their credits in any manner they like. And that is seven billion consumers with the ability to consume. (why there will be a need to be resource caps to prevent rampant consumption of useless crap)

Once we have consolidated all of the corporations, driven the banks out of existence and converted the existing governments, what could people possibly spend their money on? We will still produce, just in a different light. We will mine the landfills of the world and re-consume those resources. No resource will ever be thrown in the trash again. In fact, there will be no such thing as a trash can in the new world. None! Corporations will still exist, just with an eye to making products that will last for generations or can easily be recycled. We have enough resources already produced (including what we have thrown away) to build televisions, phones, and God only knows what else. Who knows what products lie in our future.

By acknowledging that everyone on the planet is worth at least 320 resource credits per week (based on 40 hours of productivity) and limiting that to nine months of the year, we still create an economy of scale like the universe has never seen (maybe, the Drake equation might argue with that). Our DS system along with our new economy will free everyone on the planet to develop themselves into the best person they can become. With every person on the planet having three hundred and twenty credits to spend a week we will create an economy two hundred and fifty thousand times larger than the existing economy. Whoa! Are you sure that is right? Pretty sure, you do the math.

Imagine a tree, at the top is the singularity. Below it is the trunk which feeds the singularity, below that is the roots, which branch out to each country, to each state, to each county, to each city, to each district, to each community, to each family and finally to you, the singular individual. This will build a global consciousness, create a oneness, it will unite the families of the world into the "ONE WORLD FAMILY," because we are one family. It is time that we started to act like one.

For all of you "_ _ _ _" out there screaming, "COMMUNISM, FASCISM, etc," let me explain something. This is SINGLISM. By providing every family/person with the basic needs for survival in the modern world, along with an alternate digital self, you create an economy that will grow well beyond the 14 trillion (total world economy = trillions more in debt) dollar economy of today. This will be a positive growth system instead of the negative debt system that enslaves us now. Currently 96% of the people on the planet struggle to meet their basic needs. The difference between Singlism and Communism is that the communist system was ruled by a few elites from the top. Singlism will be ruled by everyone equally starting from the family up.

Many corporations will not survive this transition, because every entity that exists from this point forward will exist for the betterment of mankind. Those that do survive the transition will make a product or provide a service and will be based on the costs of resources consumed, plus overhead and five percent. So, corporations will be allowed to make a small profit, but there will be profit caps (to prevent exploitation) and every credit made over five percent will go back to the family, back to the resource pool. Individuals will also have credit caps to prevent another oligarchy. Upon death, estate taxes will be one hundred percent (your children are already provided for, and they will have their own credits)

Everyone will get their 320 credits a week, working or not. Why would anyone work? Many won't, but they will be shunned by their communities. If you don't contribute (unless you're no longer capable) we delete your DS. That doesn't mean you cannot buy things, in our new world people will just as soon die as have their DS deleted. Plus we can reinstate that old adage, "A man who does not work, shall not eat." Of course there are exceptions to every rule. Back to our economy of economy.

Instead of taxing the back end of a product (or service), you limit it on the front end. By that method (along with restrictions on resources based on continuing damage to the environment) you force the corporations of the world to serve the people instead of us serving them. By freeing human capital you allow for innovation. People will have time to pursue arts, crafts, electronics, or any other activity that people like to do. Some people will spend all of their free time in one of the digital universes created by our singularity. Our system will be so advanced (because we all will be a part of it), being inside the digital world will be no different from being outside. Some won't be able to handle it, so we unplug them for a while and allow our mental health professionals to help them.

I envy the younger generation that will be born five years from now, they will have a complete DS. Us older people will only have the last years of our lives in our DS. But here's the thing, when we die physically, our DS will live on. Within ten years (by open sourcing all of the worlds research) we will be able to download ourselves into an A.I and live in both planes. Of course as long as you're alive your DS will do what you do, go where you go, learn what you learn. In fact, it will be you. Weird I know. I just don't know how else to get you to understand where our technology is going. (Either in our new one family world "Eden" or in our rape the world and throw it away capitalist society.)

There are some corporations who are bumping against the edges of our new world already, Sony has made a cell phone that is completely biodegradable. I would have rather they made a phone that once you're done with it, you return it and the resources are returned to the supply chain, but they are on the right track. I digress, off topic again.

Once we have our new "one family world" and we have provided everyone with food, shelter and clothing. What are we to do with all of that excess labor? We clean up and restore our environment. I can see the people of West Virginia taking the resources created by the coal companies and using them to rebuild the mountains destroyed over the last thirty years. We have been busy trashing our environment, now we can restore it. Yes, it will take time, but we will have forever to do it. No more plastic bags littering Nigeria, no more rusted hulks in Russia's bays. No more lead tailings in Oklahoma. If we produce something, we clean up as we go. No more poisoning our children. Did you know that there isn't one baby born on the planet that doesn't have thirty toxins or more in it already? What's this going to do to future generations? They have no idea. They use BPA in plastic water bottles, and it turns male frogs female!!! What the hell is that going to do to our great grandchildren?

By basing our economy on economy, by condensing our populations, by streamlining mass transit and limiting "free roving" to vacations etc. Then we can heal our planet within a century. No need for war or millions of landmines or nukes, as all resources will belong to all people, not to a corporation, or a state or a country, but to the people. There will no longer be a need to mine uranium, no need to search for more oil, no need to ship oil around the planet while holding our breath that the next spill isn't the one that adds that final straw to the camels back. We are just one or two incidents away from the food chain collapsing, do we dare risk it?

Our corporations (yes, they are ours now) will merge into one large resource pool for us all, they will transition slowly, but they will get there, they will have no choice. Resources will be conserved in every possible way, that is the base of our new wealth. The conservation of resources is economy. We will no longer make plastics from petrochemicals, but out of natural, non-toxic biodegradable materials. Everyone on the planet will need their DS device and with that, massive amounts of storage (digital memory) capacity to preserve the DS. As a system (spread all over the world) the new network (built on top of our existing networks) will be a thousand times faster allowing your DS to travel around the globe in the blink of an eye. All information ever created will be available to everyone (with some exceptions, remember everything is layered , if your community blocks certain areas or systems, tough. Move somewhere where you can access that data if necessary). I don't think words can explain what we will be capable of in the next five years. It's just too amazing. With every mind touching every other mind on the planet and all of the information of the world available, the brilliant among us will build things we never could imagine.

What I am trying to say is that products will still get made, people will do their share for fear of being deleted or for the pride of participating. To be deleted is to have never lived. We are going to be able to build our own life after death network. Anyone who is alive five years from now will be around until mankind destroys himself or God does it for us. There will always be wants and desires, there will be two billion homes to furnish and decorate. The U.S.S.R. proved that people with resources and with nothing to buy makes for a restless native. No, we have to be extremely creative, innovative, human. No one home will be the same on the inside. We are going to bring all of our technology to bear for all.

Chapter 10 Healthcare

Healthcare will become the responsibility of everyone, starting with an unadulterated healthy diet. A diet not polluted with micro amounts of thousand upon thousands of toxic additives and preservatives. With that being said, we can leverage our technology and resources to provide excellent healthcare for everyone. Each family will have a nurse who is under a nurse practitioner who is under a doctor. In a stress free world with adequate clean food and water, the cost of healthcare will plummet because there will be fewer stress related diseases. Every university hospital, nursing school, private hospital, drug company, research center will combine their knowledge and resources to become one. (Not physically, but digitally).

As a people we can focus on preventing disease instead of treating it. Of course we will need treatment in some cases, but prevention is the key. Our second line of defense will be our DS, it will let us know when there is a problem with the physical self by constantly diagnosing our status. This information will be available to your nurse and if he/she cannot handle the issue on their level, they will defer to the nurse practitioner and so on. By using this system (along with advanced digital diagnostic systems) we can keep minor ailments out of our hospitals. That should eliminate 20% of our costs (remember, economy based on resource credits and the cost of actual resources, the cost of healthcare will drop again)

This is one of the subjects where I must defer to the people with more knowledge than myself. All I know is that we have to work on prevention rather than treatment. Our current system works on a treatment bases because that's where the money is. Now, let's talk about the second largest scam in history (right behind modern banking) and that's the insurance industry. In a Singlism system there will be no need for insurance. (I hear thousands upon thousands of people crying in their pillows right now) With all of our basic needs met regardless, why insure anything? The current system is a self inflating system. You go to a doctor and he charges you $500.00 because he knows that insurance will only pay three hundred, your left on the hook for the other two even though the doc only charges that to insure that he gets his basic fee of three hundred! Next year you go to the same doctor and he charges $600.00 because his costs have risen and he knows that insurance will pay three fifty, leaving you on the hook for two fifty! He really only wants that initial three fifty. He knows that some of his patients won't pay the difference and he doesn't care, although he will sell that debt to someone else. Speaking of insurance, I think it's strange that the people who claim to have the most faith, have the most insurance.

Last year I had to have some blood work done, the cost was thirty five dollars because I paid cash. If I had had insurance, the cost would have been two hundred and fifty dollars! Why? Because they want to make sure that they get at least thirty five dollars, but more than likely the insurance will pay them one twenty five. Really!!! Here's the kicker, the insurance company knows that that test only cost thirty five dollars. So why do they pay the one twenty five? Because they have to justify those huge premiums and high deductibles, and they are really in the money business, they could care less about health care. This kind of thing happens in all sectors of our current system, from an $8.00 aspirin to a $2500.00 MRI. These costs aren't based on anything tangible, they are based on what they can get from the consumer.

If all of those costs were based on actual resources consumed, the costs for those same services would be almost negligible. By giving everyone the same level of service (in our new world) costs will decrease year after year as those of us who have been poisoned by capitalism die off. Yes, I have smoked like a freight train for years. Yes, I do expect the same level of care as anyone else. We cannot ban smoking or any other vice (and who's to say what a vice is?) We are going to take the assets of the tobacco companies (as well as every other entity on the planet) and use those particular assets for the benefit of those who drank the kool-aid.

A few years ago the state I live in (along with several others) sued big tobacco to recoup the costs of future healthcare needs of smokers. Try getting help with a smoking related problem. (Much less a direct link diagnoses to smoking) in any of those states. Our governments are "all about the money." Should there be profit in misery? In basic human management? In healthcare? In imprisonment? No, Capital no longer exists except in the hands of the individual. I often wonder where all of those billions went that the states got from tobacco? The ironic part of modern healthcare (as it exists today) is that most diseases and afflictions can be directly linked to corporate malfeasance or their products.

Corporations will no longer serve shareholders (sorry about your wealth, not really!) they will serve us all. They will no longer pollute a river, make children sick then sell them a cure. (What do you think multinational conglomerates do?) We will take all that they have and give it to everyone. Their knowledge, their resources, their logistical networks, their private digital networks and everything else. (Don't try to hide it from us, the whole worlds in on this!) That doesn't mean that innovators like Elon Musk or Richard Branson will be left out in the cold. They can keep their homes and an electric car or two, but they will serve the whole with their innovations, people like them need to create, this we must encourage. As long as it serves us all. I think Space X is an excellent resource, (for more reasons than one) we will need to launch satellites, space platforms, missions to mars, deflection and mining of asteroids. (And finally to take us out among the stars.)

I know, I was talking about health care. I think you get what I am saying. It's up to us all. We are one big family now, act like it. There is no need to be selfish or competitive (with the exception in trying to reduce resource needs). We still have to research, but we should learn to listen to those who know how to cure with nutrition. I believe that one tactic alone will reduce most of our health problems. We will have to see how it works out, won't we? We certainly aren't getting any healthier with the system we have now.

Chapter 11 Education

Free, The Khan Academy has seen the future of education and now we need to leverage that model. Every child should receive the basics (3R's) by the seventh grade. In fact, I think we underestimate most children and I believe that if they are seeking a challenge then it should be met. There are children who know more about computers than I ever will, there are children who are learning electronic engineering. We have to encourage that type of behavior in every child. Find their glory. Everyone has a place in society where they can be happy and do the most good for their community and the world. We develop their unique talents. And get this, within five years, they will be learning as their digital selves. They will be able to leverage mankind's knowledge to heights we never dreamed. Our partial DS will see it, but our physical selves wont. (I say partial DS because only someone who has grown up in both worlds will be whole in the digital realm, strange huh?)

Although, we will have to limit their access to the digital realm or they will wander off and get lost in there. (In their minds, because believe it or not, even though our tech creates the digital realm and that realm exists in one of our digital universes, the mind is where it's all perceived) Weirder and weirder. Also, we don't want an entire generation of professional gamers.

After seventh grade, children should be able to pursue whatever path appeals to them. That doesn't mean they are stuck on that path, just as a sophomore can change majors, a child's mind is much more flexible. A child might experiment with several different paths before they find one that fits them. By allowing FAMILY influences and interests to steer a child, we will get the best educated generation in history. Freeing children from strict curriculum will allow them to learn at a faster rate than previous generations. Don't be surprised when we have a million thirteen year-olds completing college level classes every year. Speaking of college, all schools will be combined into one. Not physically (well in each town they will) but digitally and as an entity. Education will be free to anyone who seeks it out. If an eighty year old man wants to learn algebra, then he will learn it. Granted, he will probably be in a digital classroom where a digital avatar will teach him. Your DS can exist in the system without you, and it can be cloned so that one teacher can be teaching ten thousand students at a time individually! I know, some of you don't believe a word I am saying, but trust me, if the capitalist and communists of this world don't nuke us all out of spite, we will be living in two worlds (and an infinite amount of universes, digital of course).

I wonder how many Einsteins the world has lost due to basic education? In some countries, children cannot afford to go to elementary schools due to the costs? What year is this? Are we in the fourteenth century here? We bring back the guild and apprentice systems in conjunction with standard education. That is how you speed innovation. You take a young man or woman working in a real setting doing real work while they are learning at school and they will see ways to make new things, speed processes, eliminate wasted resources or wasted movement. In the nineteenth century people were fascinated with maximizing the use of our time. Funny how we don't worry about that anymore, considering that we have so little time on earth. People are lucky if they get to circle the sun more than sixty times. Think about that! It's a big merry go round and you only get a few turns. What are you doing with your time? Are you going to allow the world to be raped and thrown away? Or are you going to stand up for your family and take control of your life? If you don't you won't believe how tight the collar will get and how short the leash will become.

Once again, I digress. Once we concentrate our populations, this will necessitate concentrating our schools. There is no need to build twenty buildings for one population. Its a waste of resources. Where I live there are about 60k people in the county and about 30k in the city. We have no less than twenty schools and I couldn't tell you how many buildings not including the university. We combine all of that and segregate the population by age. Imagine the cost savings and the reduction in resources required to educate the same population! Economies of scale. Not to mention the fact that soon we won't even need a building, the DS of the child will attend school (the child will be there to, just not physically) and he/she can do that from anywhere.

Once we are all combined and all information is open sourced, as it will be. The gains that we will make as a civilization will make the last two centuries look like the stone age by comparison. All of our schools will become one school, all research and development labs around the world become one. We have come to the point that competitiveness is no longer an asset to civilization, it has become a liability. We have consumed a massive amount of "easily obtained" resources. As they become more scarce, our only choice is to band together as one and conserve, reduce, reuse, innovate, teach, learn and be human. The other option is death, death of the planet, death of all species and finally death for us.

Chapter 12 More Education

All throughout history there have been arguments against a one world government, including in our sacred texts. They were all written from the point of view of not just a one world government, but of an oppressive, tyrannical, cruel and inhuman government. What I propose, what has to happen is a one family government controlled from the bottom up. Supposedly that's what we have now, but the proof of the contrary is everywhere you look. Last week on the national news I saw a tribute to a ten year old child who died of a rare type of bone cancer, it was touching. My point is, where is the tribute for the thousands of children who starve or are killed in wars everyday! Not to belittle the boys death, but he was lucky as he had his community to reflect his love. In third world countries, people are too busy trying to survive to take the time to stage tributes to a dead child.

Within our new world, no one in Geneva will tell you that you cannot worship on Sunday. That you cannot eat pork or that you cannot smoke, those are personal decisions. Every rule or law or restriction will be based on what is best for the community and will be decided by that community. There is an old saying that all politics is local, if that's the case, then why don't you have any say in how your community is ruled? I cannot tell you that I have all of the answers, because I don't. What I can tell you is that there are thousands of decisions to be made, including at what level in the "Chain of Councils" decisions should be made. The World Council will have no right to rule on community matters or city matters or district matters. The entire world will have a vote in deciding where decisions are made and on what level.

I would also like to say that politics is only politics when money is involved. It says in the Bible that "the love of money is the root of all evil." We have bred an entire world of money lovers, doesn't that make evil the tree? We have to cut down that tree and replace it with a tree of humanism or Singlism. I haven't really done any heavy lifting in writing this text other than to gather the ideas of a world in trouble and put them into one semi-coherent thought. We have to get over our primal fears and embrace our technological capabilities to create the world we all want. A world that we all know is possible, but that we are all scared to death to create. We fear our own destruction, which by doing nothing is guaranteed.

For a long time I believed that people weren't worth saving. I believed that every one of you deserved the destruction that is about to befall you. I wavered on this thought and it never really changed. What I didn't want to see was the destruction of the natural world and the creatures that live within it. Just what makes humans so sacrosanct that they deserve to live at the expense of the rest of the world? In fact, I would have gladly gone first if I could take the rest of you with me. (I know, a bit harsh) Then one day about a month ago I asked my mother if people were worth saving. She told me that she had to believe that or she couldn't go on. She says that people are inherently good. With that said, I have a large family and I wouldn't want anything to happen to them. I don't want my family to die a fiery death by nukes. So, I decided to write this to give the world a chance.

For a long time, I prayed that God would wipe us all out and leave the world in peace. I was sincere. I don't think that is his plan however, I think it was up to my family to redeem me. I look around and I see dead zones in the ocean. Another species goes extinct every day. The worlds forests are turned into cheap furniture and cardboard. I see oceans of litter all over our once pristine landscape. When I was about fourteen I became obsessed with finding a spot on the planet where I could look and see nothing man made. I told my father about it and he said, there is nowhere you can go to see that. I thought he was wrong, but he wasn't. In the most remote areas of Antarctica, you can find nuclear fallout from seventy years of "testing." (well you might not be able to "see" it, but it's there.) In the middle of the ocean you can find toothbrushes and umbrella handles. We have trashed the place, we live on one huge landfill. Honestly, I don't think that people can trust each other enough to join together into the one family that they are. I hope I am wrong, but if not, each and everyone of you has doomed our race by doing nothing.

Throughout this text I have avoided mentioning God and

religion to keep your mind from screaming "fanatic." By avoiding God, we avoid ourselves. God resides in all consciousness and that as a whole, (a singular consciousness) people will always do what is right. (I believe Muhammad said something very similar in the Quran.) Yes, I sort of quoted Muhammad, but here's the thing, we have to respect every religion. Respect, justice and freedom is the way to secure the future for all of us. Can you say that one religion is better or more sincere than another? Without Islam's contributions to science we might well still be in the iron age. Each religion and each group of people have made their own contributions to the world we live in. It may be true that our path has strayed and we are destroying our world, but only as a family can we change that.

Back to our arguments, I have come to the conclusion that if we want to save our world for our families and future generations, then we will literally have to go through hell to get there. The singularity is both our salvation and our damnation. Our singular consciousness is strengthening daily via our vast communication networks, which is also our weakness. Those who want to retain their wealth, their power and their Nation States will stop at nothing to prevent us from becoming one family. Why do you think that a one world government has been demonized for centuries? There is some truth to those stories, if we allow our current system to continue with their version of a one world government, we will remain slaves. We will all die in an ocean of blood. If you think for one minute that a one world government doesn't already exist, then you are blind. It used to be that there were two governments, the communists and the capitalists. But they have joined together in order to rape the world faster and concentrate their wealth while the rest of us bear the burden of their "success."

Before 2012 there was speculation that our world would end. There were stories and shows all pointing to the worlds demise or a change in consciousness. What those stories and shows couldn't see was that through our networks, the singularity was developing. Thoughts fly around the world in the blink of an eye. Governments (which are little underlings of the real powers) fell simply because the "mind" of the people was connected. There is a singularity and it grows every day. By joining together as one family, we can complete the singularity and all benefit from it. Or we can allow the rapists of the world to remain in power. One way we all die, the other way some of us have a chance. Yes, there is an apocalypse (the lifting of the veil, the dissemination of hidden knowledge) and seems like we should have seen it before now.

What I find interesting is that all of those stories were focused on the date of 21/12. That is why I am releasing/publishing this on December the Twenty First of Two Thousand and Thirteen. It's all about the numbers. (I won't get into that, everything in the Universe is based on math) To me it's like the scene in the Matrix where Neo (or whatever his name was) looks down the hall and then all of a sudden he sees the underlying code. It was a lot like that when it hit me on November the 26th. Strange I know, but by this or a similar method can we save our world. I don't think the actual date of Dec. 21st 2012 had anything to do with the revelation, but it's funny that the Mayans said we would enter a new age at this time. I only wish that I could know how it all ends.

Why do we have to change? Take an average person who does everything right. They get good grades at school, graduate, go to college, get married, buys a home, has children and then takes care of their aging parents. Now they are in the home stretch of life and about to retire. However, fate has a different plan for him/her. They become ill, or their spouse does. Insurance pays the first 60% of the costs, but they won't pay for the treatment that will save their life. They struggle at first, using their retirement funds, then they end up selling their home, their cherished possessions and then the next thing you know, they are broken. No home, no retirement funds and at the mercy of the state. They get by in a rental or in one of their child's homes, but now they have to work until they no longer can. They are eventually separated and regulated to a state run nursing home where they are just another body taking up space. We all are going to go downhill (unless we get our tech together and learn how to keep the physical body alive forever) but how we live the last years of our lives shouldn't be at the mercy of money.

I could have changed that example in a thousand different ways, one of them could have gotten treatment and become addicted to their pills. (which happens much more often than you might think) Or some Wall Street twerp could have lost their retirement. Also, with America's new laws, the insurance company couldn't have canceled their policy, however there is no law preventing the insurance company from raising the rates until they can no longer afford it. How is it we live in a world where someone has to choose between medicine and food. Either way their health suffers.

Let's look at our argument from another angle. Obama and his first (and second) campaigns for President were all about "hope and change." This is what most Americans voted for, change. Change you can believe in! Right? Honestly I think Obama had good intentions, but he was naive. Since his administration took power, they used all of their political capital to pass one bill. The Obama-care laws. His bill was originally fair to the people, but he caved in order to get it passed. By the time this legislation was passed it was watered down and pandered to the insurance companies. All it did was guarantee them a customer base. Now he has caved to private interests at every turn, he wanted to promote clean energy, now he's in the pocket of "dirty energy" meaning big oil. The military industrial complex has expanded it's war on "terror" to every corner of the globe. Didn't he want to end the wars, stop the bloodshed?

Do not be fooled, we are seeing the beginning of World War IV. (yes four) Remember the cold war? That was world war three, remember Vietnam? Russia in Afghanistan? (you know the Russians laugh their asses off every time our excursion in Afghanistan is mentioned) Why have they expanded the "war" to every corner of the globe? They are centralizing control of the few who control our planet. They cannot have anyone dissenting. Drone strikes are a form of pre-crime assassination. I am not saying that there aren't bad people out there who will kill innocent people, there are. But let's be honest here, my country (the United States of America) re-invented total war. It was a common practice in the mid-ages, but as the world matured battles were fought by soldiers on a field of battle.

During the Civil War, Robert E. Lee invaded the North, he wouldn't allow his soldiers to touch the civilian population. He tolerated the civilians coming into the Confederate camps to taunt his men. The North on the other hand made war on everyone in the South, it was the beginning of total war. (Now don't get me wrong, the policies of the Southern aristocracy were wrong) The United States has no problem making war on an entire population. In fact, I wouldn't be surprised if a drone doesn't find me once this is published.

I have to say that I love my country, but if the world wants to survive, we have to choose our families and our planet over the existing nation states. My country is ruled by a handful of people with massive amounts of cash at their disposal. I am sure that they sleep fine at night after a steak dinner. While the people who make those resources worth something have to depend on government assistance to eat. I have strayed off topic, but it has to be said.

What do the terrorist of the world really want? Some want to expand their religion, some believe that their religion is under attack. Some want independent states, some want power. Obviously there are those who are just evil and will destroy for the thrill of destroying. But if you look at it in a different light. Most want to live the way they want while ensuring a secure, productive home for their families. We can all have that, we can all respect the beliefs of our neighbors and their families. Once we take "money" out of the issues facing the world and focus on our resources, there will be little reason to incite terror in others. There will always be extremists from every religion, some use terror, some use money, some use their power to advance their beliefs. Those we will deal with in their turn. Communities will deal with their own and those that won't we will deal with them.

With a single global consciousness, we will be like any other individual. We will be of two or three minds on any given subject. A vast majority of people might override another section of the people concerning their beliefs, but that doesn't mean they have a right to force those beliefs on them. Beliefs will not be on the negotiation table in any council. What you believe and how you act is no ones concern unless you hurt another human. That is the whole point of having a "Chain of Councils" so that disputes are dealt with on a level appropriate to the issue. I am sure that the people of the world can find a balance of belief. I see the biggest problems of the "hive" being a difference of belief, all they have to remember is that it doesn't matter what God you do or don't believe in. How do you know that Allah isn't God isn't Ishnu isn't Yahweh? We have to look past our differences and embrace our humanity, our family.

There are Liberals, Conservatives, Socialists, Communists, Christians, Israelis, Islamist, Leftists, Reactionaries, Anarchists and any number of a thousand different labels. What all of those labels overlook is that we are all human. We are human beings, simple. I don't think I can say it any better. HUMAN BEINGS. That is BE ING, we are, we live, we have this beautiful blue marble to play and work upon. It seems that all anyone wants to do is undermine someone else who doesn't have the same label as them. Pitiful. We must accept our differences while EMBRACING our HUMANISM. That is Singlism. There is an advantage of having a single consciousness. It's here now, we just haven't connected all of humanity yet. We will and when we do, we can truly know peace.

Traditionally, my family are Democrats (for the most part, my grandfather on my mothers side was a staunch

Republican.) As I grew up and learned the difference between the two, I decided that I was a Conservative Republican. The more I learned of the Republican Party the more I realized that I was too conservative for them. Republicans are really only conservative with their own money, just as Democrats are only liberal with someone elses. I had a friend who used to say that he was neither a liberal republican nor a socialist democrat. The truth of both parties is that they only play up their differences when there is an election. They are both two sides of the same coin. They agree on the fundamentals of capitalism. That is why there are never any real changes in policy from one administration from another. They agree on the wholesale rape of the planet for the sole benefit of less than 1% of the population.

Early man worshiped God and by proxy nature which they saw as the manifestation of God. Nature provides for us and in return we destroy her. People all over the world today worship retail, they find divinity in plastic crap at their local retail establishment. Oh, there are those who go to churches, synagogues, temples or mosques. When they leave their temples they go out to where their heart really lies and they buy, buy, buy. I am not saying that we cannot have nice things, I am saying that each of those things come at a price that cannot be monetized. Consumerism has become the new mantra. Look at my new car, my new house, my new phone. That car has a carbon footprint the size of Atlanta, the house came at a cost of a quarter acre of jungle and that phone, it costs in an incalculable way. (When is the last time you had a conversation with someone that didn't look at their phone every five seconds.) The plastics will never go away, the heavy metals will leach into the groundwater. (once its trashed and buried) The amount of waste created every year from unwanted or outdated electronics is huge. Very little of that waste is recycled and usually when it is recycled its done in a terrifying manner. Children in China stand around fires of toxic burning plastic in order to get a couple of grams of metal. Horrifying.

Like many of my fellow Americans, I bought the lie (or temptation) of "sex, drugs and rock and roll." This is a deliberate message created by the mass media to "dumb down" society. Schools no longer teach civics or real history. Over the last forty years America has been extremely successful in exporting this lie. Kids all over the world aspire to be "American" by smoking, drinking, drugging while banging their heads. Some say blue jeans and the Beatles brought down the Berlin wall. Not true, another lie. What brought down the wall was cheap oil, it bankrupted the U.S.S.R. I wonder if the Saudi's knew what instability that one act would bring to the world, if they would have cooperated with the Bush family to lower the price of oil in the eighties.

The truth behind this lie, like so many others, was to bring the U.S. down to second world status while lifting up the rest of the world. Strange but true. The capitalists saw that they could make more money if they expanded their markets and lowered wages. They started by enacting NAFTA which lowered some wages and a few factories moved to Mexico. Which was good for Mexico and I really didn't have a problem with that. Then our buddy Clinton petitioned in favor of allowing China into the World Trade Organization making China a "free trade zone." He petitioned with the argument that our products would have all of these new consumers to buy our products. (Remember I am writing from an

American's point of view) What happened instead was that China devalued their "currency" which made their labor extremely cheap. Which allowed them to flood our markets with "cheap" products.

This attracted huge investment in factories, drawing jobs away from the U.S. and Mexico at a rate never seen in history. The last time there was that much loss of industry was when the U.S. got into mills and basically destroyed that industry in England. I digress. What we have now is a trade war. It's the first salvo in a war that will eventually lead to armed conflict. One day China will want it's cash, except they will no longer take our bonds. We have been selling them paper in trade for their environment. With every interest payment due to them we give them more paper. We do this with all our debts because all our "cash" is debt.

Now I really don't care if China makes a product or if India makes it, every man on the planet has a right to a good job and a healthy home. But we don't have that, do we. What we have is slave wage jobs with poisoned food, poisoned water and plastic crap. This is progress? This is a BOOMING economy? How is it that the more resources we squander, the better our economy? Want to know why America's economy is failing? There is a disconnect between Wall Street and the rest of America. The numbers that go up and up are based on profits made from products made in another country. General Electric should be traded on the Chinese Stock Exchange rather than in New York. If that reality ever hits home with Americans, (which it will) the shit will truly hit the fan.

Never mind, everything on Wall Street is an illusion of wealth, the true wealth lies in humanity and if we don't clean up our source of life, we are all screwed. If I were to show you a basketball and I had you take a sharpie and color it black then I told you that it represented the Earth. That the layer of ink you put on it was about a thousand times thicker than the layer of life on our planet, would you believe me? No? Well it is true, the layer of life on this world is extremely thin. Life begets life, you cannot eat anything that hasn't been alive. You can drink water which was never alive, but it is full of life and is the harbinger of life. The layer of life goes from about a foot under your feet to the top of the trees, that's it, there is no more. Once it's destroyed or a species dies out, it's over. (Maybe one day we can bring them back, but with our current capitalist system it wont happen unless there is money in it. Maybe they will develop an extinct species zoo?) Life is the only thing that can feed you, I don't know how to put it any simpler.

The corporations however are feeding you petrochemicals and thousands of other laboratory creations that extend "shelf life" or sweeten or whatever. We are not designed to eat that crap. Right now we are all one huge experiment in a mad scientist laboratory, and he has no idea what he's doing. WE THE PEOPLE (all of us, everyone on the planet) has to take charge of our lives. That means taking charge of everything.

Extending on the loss of jobs and income in America, ten years ago I was making on average twenty to twenty five dollars an hour, then politics stepped in and allowed tens of thousands of Mexicans to overrun our borders and take those jobs for a quarter of what we earned. Which I do not blame the Mexicans for, who I blame are the master capitalist who played us off of each other. I can remember being on a highrise in Nashville and the animosity between the groups was palatable. Money separated us, in our new world humanity will bring us together. I have nothing personal against any man who is trying to do better for his family. If I had been born in Mexico and I needed to feed my family, I would jump a fence, cross a desert, because that is what you do for family. But the real truth behind that story is the fact that there should not be economic inequality on two different sides of the damn fence. What the hell do we need fences for, we are one family. (Yes, and I will continue to say it)

Borders only separate and divide us. I know that I am not making any friends here, but think about this. Would you leave home if you didn't have to? In our new world, there will be no reason to go to another part of the world to make a living. The only reason for a Mexican to come to Tennessee will be to go to the Opry. Economic inequality is WRONG. It allows one group of people to exploit another group. The Mexicans who come here are paid crap and most of that money goes back home, leaving the individual who earned it living in poverty. Why do you think they live ten to an apartment or that you see eight guys in a Volkswagen?

Consider this, the job I used to do pays about $12.00 to $14.00 today if you're lucky. That may sound like a lot to some people (especially those who live on less than two dollars a day, which most do) but if you consider the average person in the U.S. has to pay for housing, transportation, food, insurance, water, electricity, health care and on top of that, an ass load of taxes. Really? I often wonder how people on minimum wage live! It's just too much to take care of, but why is it like this? Because the system is designed to keep the average man from gaining any true wealth. I can hear it now, this guy is some loser who just couldn't make it in our world. I will have you know that on my best year I CLEARED over a hundred grand and probably got close to hundred and fifty. Ask the IRS, they will confirm it. Which after I publish this, that will probably be the excuse the government uses to lock me up forever. Whatever. Back to the point.

If you know anything about the markets, you know that every seven years or so they take a huge dump. Why? Because of the master capitalists, when they start dumping stocks, the followers follow. Then the master capitalists swoop in and buy up all of the resources at bargain basement prices. Don't believe me? Look at 2008 when GM stock was kicked off the (NYSE) exchange and listed on the over the counter bulletin board, it was selling for less than a dollar. Today it lists for forty dollars. Think there isn't some master of money out there that didn't see that and take advantage. Imagine the resources that GM has, they were the largest car manufacturer in the world. (Of course they won't be making cars anymore, maybe pods?)

Why did the economy nearly crash in 2008? Because investors started using homes as investments. The price of homes didn't go up because there were more people out there needing homes. (there were, but they couldn't afford them) It was a huge ponzi scheme, investors move in and buy a home, they turn around and sell that home to another investor and the first guy goes out and buys another, this merry go round of home buying and selling drove the cost of housing out of the average man's reach. Then the investors realized that they had too many homes and that they had to put some people in them. With a wink and a nod people who couldn't afford homes were sold homes. This resulted in driving up home costs again. Then one day someone in a bank somewhere in New York realizes it's all B.S. and that they lost the game of hot potato and were holding all the paper. It wasn't that simple, but it was.

Investment almost destroyed the economy five years ago. Want to hear the scary part? It's happening all over again. Except this time investors are holding all the paper. They are overloaded with homes that they cannot sell. Oh, they are doing the merry go round thing again, but the thing is, what they are doing (although it might benefit them in the short term) is wrong. Every time an investor buys a home to make a profit, they lift that home up out of the reach of some couple just starting out. Or a middle class family that's lived in rentals for fifteen years while saving for a down payment. Every year those people wait, their cash that they saved is worth less, less at the store, less in the marketplace, just less. What a booming economy.

It all goes to reinforce my point, an economy based on debt and the squandering of resources is not an economy. I often wonder how the professional economists see the world.

Do they look at a waterfall for it's beauty or do they see a site for a mill? Earlier I said that we have to redefine capital, and we have. We also decided that every man (and woman) is worth 320 resource credits per week. That breaks down to about $5.36 per hour. And I was just bitching about twelve. We are changing to a resource based economy where before everything else, we take care of the people. Then we do other things. Five dollars and change an hour is a fortune if you don't have to pay for housing, electric, water, etc etc etc.

People in the United States love to bitch about foreign aid, "billions to that nation and billions more to that one, they don't deserve it" What most Americans don't realize is that the foreign aid we send is a kick back. For every billion in aid sent to a country, we are exploiting that country for ten. Who pays the price for that. It's not just the U.S. that does this, I am sure England and France and Russia and China all have a piece of the World Bank. The sweet World Bank and the International Monetary Fund. What a joke. These guys go into a country and loan them huge amounts of money that they have to spend how they are told. The "creditors" know damn well that this country or nation cannot pay it back, it takes up all of their income to pay the interest. So once a said country defaults, the IMF and WB comes in and takes their resources. You got coal, we'll take that, you got fishing grounds, we'll take that, you got oil, we'll take that. And who suffers? The local population that cannot drink their own water because coke bought the rights from the IMF for a tenth of their actual worth. Really, this is economy? I know that some of you reading this just don't care, and that's alright because no one will care when they come to take what's yours. I own my home and everything I have outright, but that doesn't mean that the government cannot take it. If they want it they just raise the taxes to a point where I cannot pay them. It happened here in the South before, right after the Civil War. Carpetbaggers swept across the land and took what they wanted. It will happen again unless we ALL unite into one, one consciousness, one family, ONE.

Chapter 13 Almost There?

I can preach forever and if you don't get it, then you don't get it. We have one planet, it cannot hide from those who would destroy it. If we want to save it, then Singlism is the one answer. (I haven't heard any others) I have another twenty or thirty pages of arguments for one reason or another, but as I rewrite and re-edit, I don't think that ten thousand pages is enough to convince some of you. There are a lot of you who will dig in and say never, you will be run over. Think the military's of the world will be able to stomach the wholesale slaughter of people who just want what's best for their families? They might fight for a while, but many will turn, most will turn. There will be blood (to quote a movie title) one way or another. I hope that people will see the sense in what I am saying and just change, I know, I am a lot like you. Patriotic, but what do men really fight for? They fight for their families and the land that those families occupy.

No one wants to take away your country, there will be no invasion of foreign forces trying to change you by force. This isn't radical Islam where if you're an infidel we cut off your head. This is a family trying to heal itself. One, one with each other, one with nature and one with God. OK. I know some of you don't believe in God, that's OK., do you believe in life, in family? We want the earth to heal, to take a step back and say, OK we have gone too far, what do we have to do to fix it. This is about family, about nature, about love. (was trying to avoid that word as well, it's just too soft a connotation)

No one will be able to escape the singularity, there will be a single consciousness, the question is, will you be a part of it? What we have now is merely part of the singularity. You can see it and hear it, it exists in the way an opinion flies around the planet. The way a story is told to everyone almost at once. The true singularity is the point where technology and mankind meet, become one and prosper. Sci-fi would have you believe (and they may not be wrong) that our technology will become a singularity outside of mankind, then decide that mankind is either a threat or useless then decides to destroy us. By linking all of mankind together via our DS (digital selves) we will create a singularity, a consciousness that will be the superior of any software based singularity. Our combined consciousness will be a true reflection of God. I am curious what scientist will say, is it possible to have two singularities? I know that there will be one made of all of us, I guess now it's a race to see which one is first. I don't think it's a race that we can afford to lose.

Personally, I just got sick and tired of the rat race. In order to get ahead in our society, someone else has to step back or be stepped on. When I had my own business, I couldn't sleep at night. I was worried all of the time. If you're not on top of your business all of the time, it will unravel. The worst part was the fact that grown men acted like third graders. Not because they were immature, but because they were constantly trying to prove their worth at the expense of another employee. It's how were programmed, everything is a competition. There used to be a rather popular bumper sticker here in the 80's that said, "The guy who dies with the most toys wins!" Really, it's all about the toys? Yeah, it is. Too bad, it should be all about the family.

I find that the villages of the pre modern age (even with all of their problems and lack of medicine) had one of the most idyllic lives possible. Each man, woman and child knew that they were responsible for themselves and their family. Even though they had themselves to worry about, they took care of each other. If someone needed a barn, they gathered together to build it. If someone was in danger, they banded together to meet the threat. Look to how the iditarod began, a village was in danger so their neighbors and friends risked their lives for the lives of others. That is a rare trait among modern men. Yes, the Red Cross goes all over the world to help people, but they have modern transportation and their lives are rarely at risk. Back to my point, I dropped out of the rat race, just said screw it, it's not worth it. I thought I was alone, then a week or two ago I read an article in Businessweek (I think it was Businessweek) that said that 91 million Americans have dropped out. This leaves only 63% of the population to carry the load. This is the lowest rate of employment in the U.S. since the 70's, since before women joined the workforce in mass.

This is just another argument for Singlism. People don't drop out because they are lazy or because they don't want to work. They drop out because it's no longer worth it. Wages have been decimated in all levels of the workforce. The middle class has joined the lower class. Imagine a guy who has worked at IBM for thirty five years and he gets a layoff notice. He cannot find another job because we just don't hire "mature" people. Two years later he's on government assistance and wonders where he went wrong. He didn't go wrong anywhere, politics and capitalism just moved on and left him behind. It happens every day to someone somewhere. Not just America, everywhere.

What could be a better argument for Singlism. The same guy in the new world can look over all of the new "open sourced" information and innovate on a project started in the seventies in Japan. He looks at that information through a different perspective from the people who originally worked on it and discovers a way to download your consciousness into our network. Oh, it will happen, but in our new world, it will happen a lot faster. These are the people who our children should look up to. Rock stars, actors and athletes have their place in our society, but they are poor role models. How many times has an athlete turned out to be a "human." What were they thinking being human. We put these people on pedestals, but they are extremely narrow pedestals. Our heroes should be the builders, the innovators, the engineers and technicians who make our world work.

Chapter 14 Transportation

Our transportation system is huge waste of resources. It divides our land, kills our wildlife and the cost is outrageous. Depending on where an interstate is built it can cost anywhere from a million dollars a mile to three hundred million a mile. Once it's built it has to be maintained and on top of that every vehicle that goes down that interstate pays up to .45 cents per mile to go over it. That doesn't even count the costs of millions of vehicles, billions of tires, billions of gallons of motor oil. Then there are the tens of thousands of animals killed by traffic, the tens of millions of gallons of weed killers sprayed, the billions of tons of salt and other chemicals sprayed on top of that. It's resource intensive and requires more and more resources to continue using. Am I the only one who thinks that counter intuitive?

What we need is a solution similar to what a company called EC3 is working on. High speed vehicles in vacuum tubes, from any one city in the world to another in 42 minutes.

The best part is that you only have to build it once. In our new world we will build in the most economical way possible with the thought that whatever we are building must last hundreds upon hundreds of years. Don't laugh, there are roads and aqueducts built by the Romans over two thousand years old. They knew that if you build it right the first time, it will pay for itself over and over and over again.

Well, why don't we build interstates that last forever? Politics. They will tell you that it's too expensive to build for the long term. Truth is that they want to keep the excavators and the paving companies working. Remember, they have to keep the "economy" going. I almost laugh every time I say "economy" in the context of the capitalist system. It's pure waste. Imagine our new transportation systems high in the air speeding over a natural world. Between the continents we build these high pressure vacuum tubes thirty foot in diameter to carry people and resources under the oceans in just a few hours. No more need for fuel extensive jumbo jets. Not to say that technology cannot be of a use to us. We will have a space program after all, we might need a fuel powered jet to help us build a space elevator. Oh, there will be one. In a resource based economy we will be able to afford it or a similar system.

Local transportation will be as simple and as affordable as we can make it. We don't have to burn fuel to move. We burn enough fuel to move hundreds of people just to go to the store. Waste. I know, you think you will lose your freedom and not be able to travel in our new world. That's where you're wrong, if you have the time (which you will working nine months or less per year) you can walk outside your home, catch your local transport to your cities transport hub and be anywhere in the world in less than a day. The best part is that it won't cost you a dime. Our world is a world where humanity is the most important variable. It will no longer be all about the dollar.

The biggest challenge or project ahead of us will be dismantling the world we live in now. We will have to use the existing system while we build our one family world. The good part of that is that it gives us an affordable (in terms of environmental damage and the fact we don't have to reproduce those resources) resource base to work from. Every brick, every two by four and every square inch of asphalt will be resourced for our cities. I would be comfortable saying that in the U.S. there is enough asphalt to build half the world a new home. Yes, we can use it. I was working on a sci-fi story once and in the story there is a castle built out of thousands upon thousands of tomb stones. I wouldn't be surprised that if anyone survives the capitalist world (if we fail to destroy it) they will use any and all resources at hand. Once again, I have strayed.

My point was that transportation doesn't have to destroy and divide. It doesn't require more and more resources and capital to keep it going. During the cold war the Soviets had a subway system that was the envy of the world. It had crystal chandeliers and was reminiscent of a king court. Mass transportation doesn't have to be trash transportation. Once we indoctrinate our future generations in a proper manner to respect one another and nature, it will be like it was when airplanes were first used for transport. Up until the mid-seventies when people went to the airport, they dressed like they were going to church. Now I am not saying that we have to enforce a dress code, but people dress according to their culture. Back in the twenties, the thirties and the forties, criminals dressed like they worked in a bank. Now we are blue jeans and tee shirt slobs. (I am one of them, it's comfortable, what can I say)

Attitude is everything. If people are in a culture that respects others, they respect themselves. There were once hundreds of styles of dress around the world, it has all been reduced to jeans and tees. That is a direct result of our exported lie. Yeah, I am a bastard. The point is that a cultures dress is a direct reflection of how they see themselves. In the thirties the emperor of Japan visited Britain, while there he went to the best of tailors and had suits made for him. Then he proceeded to dress in that fashion from that point on. The shame of that incident is the princes of England wore the native Japanese fashion to a party after the visit in order to make fun of the Emperor. I believe the quote was something about monkeys in suits. Really?

What is messed up about that is the business suit has infiltrated every culture in the world. People feel that if they want to be taken seriously they have to dress like the western countries. We have exported shame of culture. Do you think the President of China would feel comfortable meeting another leader while wearing hanfu? I love to stray off topic. In our new world, culture will be encouraged to localize once again.

Dismantling our cities will be a start, there are homes spread or sprawled all over the planet. Concentration of population is necessary. That doesn't mean that we will destroy every building outside of our new cities. There will be many that will be wonderful vacation spots for families and couples to get away from the norm. Hunting cabins will be left in remote areas, yes we will keep our guns. There is no need to ban them. With everyone living two lives, one in the physical world and another in the digital world, you couldn't get away with murder if you wanted to. Everything will be recorded and uploaded to the system in real time.

No, no one will be able to hack the system. Cross stability, it will work much like bitcoin works today. Every system will cross check every other system. If someone tries to destabilize the system, the system will identify and lock out that user. Not to mention the thought of being deleted. It will be feared almost as much as death. Yeah, it sounds crazy, but it will happen and you can either embrace it or fight it. I would suggest embracing it unless we fail and the capitalist system triumphs. Then you better run to the edge of the earth or you will not only be a slave, but a slave with a very short leash.

I have to touch on this next issue, our system not only wastes huge amounts of resources but we flush or bury everything we use. Life is meant to be recycled. How else can you explain vultures and flesh eating beetles. Everything on the planet has always went just as the Bible said, ashes to ashes, dust to dust. The meaning of life, is life. What we do is bury everything. All of the nutrients that we consume in a lifetime will either be absorbed or flushed. Either way they end up buried for all time, out of the chain of life. Every resource we use in our homes (including our homes) either end up in flames or in a landfill. Look at the resources that belong to the Earth that we have taken away and locked up out of her reach. What this does is take more and more resources out of life. Our bodies were not meant to be buried under six feet of earth out of the reach of life. Because we take ourselves out of the chain of life, we are truly dead.

We should go from being dead and buried to being part of something else. Maybe part of a vulture or a fungus or a beetle. Now I am not endorsing leaving corpses laying around. What I am endorsing is one of two options. (And with innovation I am sure there are many others.) One, you would be fed to flesh eating beetles and then your family could entomb your bones in a family crypt. Two, if you're more enlightened, your body could be placed in a high bacteria, high pressure and high temperature cauldron and turned into fuel. I know, it kind of sounds creepy, but to be buried away from the rest of life is just wrong. The Jewish people bury their dead in coffins that are designed to allow the body to disintegrate. They still lock those nutrients away from life however.

To broach another subject, in our new world, there will be no trash. No landfills, everything will be recycled for the resources. Everything. We will also embark on a quest to mine the existing landfills (while trapping the methane produced) and recover the millions of tons of resources that have been buried. Napoleon II had silverware made of aluminum,at the time it was the most expensive metal on the planet. I wonder what he would think of us burying tons of it everyday? Resources cost us and the planet way too much to be squandered. With the appropriate approach we have enough readily available resources to meet our requirements. (That's even with us building a billion homes during the same period.)

The world that we live in now is based on petrochemicals, fertilizers produced from petrochemicals and plastic crap (also made from petrochemicals.) If we continue on our current path, our existing reserves of oil will be more or less depleted by 2060. (this is based on the rapid rise of India and China, the world's oil was formerly only utilized by the U.S. and Western Europe.) By transitioning to a pure electrical energy environment, we can stretch (and even build on) our oil reserves, allowing them to last for the next thousand years. Without an immediate change in consciousness and attitude, the lack of resources will be nothing less than catastrophic. With fewer reserves of resources, nations will have no other choice than to war for those reserves. They will do so for their countries, for their communities, for their families. I will for mine, so why shouldn't they for theirs? Hence the rising military budgets around the world.

All of this seems to be a pipe dream. In fact, if I wasn't writing this, I would question every word. It sounds as if there is no possible way to organize the people and resources of the world to accomplish such a lofty goal. That is where you would be wrong. People have always risen to the challenge when their lives depended on it. Back in WWII there were more resources brought together in the shortest time period ever, in order to defend or offend another country. In the United States one of the most important issues facing the country was air power. Without air superiority, the war would have been lost, PERIOD. In order to achieve their goal, all of the airplane manufactures suspended competition, open sourced all information and acted as one entity. Without this sacrifice of "capitalism" I would dare say that more than likely I would be writing in German today, if at all. Which makes my point for me, if we want to survive as a race, we must sacrifice capitalism, along with communism, socialism and most importantly dictatorships and monarchies.

I know that I go along way around a subject and through several others to make a point and to get to that point, I am just going to come out and say it. We expend enormous amounts of resources to accomplish what a few well spent ones can achieve. We don't have to have a resource sucking transportation system, the only real purpose of which is to make us "feel" free. What seems like freedom, (driving 80 mph with the windows down) is actually one of the strongest links in the chain that is slavery. Enough said on the subject, either you get it, or you don't.

Chapter 15 Transition

We will have to dismantle our existing cities and the infrastructure that supports them in order to achieve our goal of a resource based economy. (What I mean by a resource based economy is a resource neutral economy, there is no need to rape the Earth further to support our worlds people.) Detroit city for example has recently declared bankruptcy. She has lost her manufacturing base and with it, the people who made it possible. Detroit has tens of thousands of abandoned homes throughout its city. The city, in response to these empty hulks, has taken it upon itself to crush these homes and bury their remains.

Huge amounts of resources gone, the trees that made the lumber for those homes are gone, you can grow more, but those are gone. The asphalt that made up their shingles, gone.

The stone, block and concrete that made up their foundations, their fireplaces and their facades, gone. Oh, we can mine the landfills where these materials were entombed, but we will have to use even more resources to reclaim resources which were recently at our fingertips. Does this make sense to you?

What we will have to do to get to where we want to be is to convert one county, (here in the U.S., it may be approached differently in your country) one city at a time. We cannot tear up a road until we have alternative transport for a community. It's not like we can just tear it all down all at once, if we tried such an approach, people would starve by the billions. We have to keep our massive monoculture farms alive until they are no longer needed. City by city, county by county, state by state it can be done. If I was in charge I would take the largest city along with a medium size city and the smallest town in a state and start with them. Once they were transformed (new homes for all in a central location, a sustainable food system in place and a resource neutral transport system in place) then I would do it all over again with the next largest, medium and smallest. While I was working on these cities and towns, I would also be working on replacing the countries transportation system. I am not sure who said it, but Rome wasn't built in a day. However, unless we start, we will never achieve our goal.

Want to address the elephant in the room? (speaking of which, if I caught you poaching, I would disappear you and your entire family. If you want people to observe the rules, you have to have the harshest of penalties.) We have large standing armies all over the world. These armies (navies, air-forces and marines) all exist to "defend" us from one another. There are countries in South America with a large military that have never fought in a war and have little or no chance of being invaded. Back to my point, our world's military's do little more than consume the vastest amount of resources of any other entity on the planet. (the U.S. uses more oil than any country, that's a given, right? what you may not know is that the U.S. military consumes 2% of that oil, which would mean that they consume more oil than most countries.) (In 2007, they consumed more oil than 158 other countries, not combined, that is the only year I could find data for.)

What our military's are good for is resource gathering and

distribution. No one manages (or miss-manages, depending on your viewpoint) resources more efficiently than the military's of the world. There is no need to destroy their institutions, their customs or their legacies. They are really good at turning children into adults. In our new world, we will need men/women of good character, high honor and a sense of duty to family. In fact, I would venture to say that every young man and woman at the age of 18 should be required to spend a minimum of two years serving in one of our institutions. They should be turned into physically fit, morally fit responsible adults. Then again, who am I to say.

The basic lesson that we should have learned from history is that no people will feel secure as long as their neighbor has a gun pointed at their head. To feel secure, they get themselves a gun and point it back in turn. We learned (or re-learned) this lesson at the beginning of the Cold War. The Soviets did not sleep well when the U.S. had nukes and they did not. Which was the grounds for half our battle with the Soviets during said war. Once the Soviets armed themselves with nukes, we had to have bigger nukes. This game of one-up-man ship lasted for forty-five years and I am not sure that it has ended yet, in one form or the other. On a personal note, whenever I move to a new neighborhood I take out my guns and shoot for a few hours. Just to let my neighbors know that I am armed and know how to use them. MAD or mutually assured destruction is insanity, period. As more and more countries obtain nukes, it's just a matter of time before another one gets used. I hope it's not on your city.

Which brings us to the huge stores of military grade uranium along with energy grade uranium stock piled over the face of our planet. Not to mention all of the other radioactive substances we have concentrated (and continue to concentrate) and distribute. Here in the U.S. we currently store our used radioactive substances on site of our nuclear power plants. Even after 70 years of production and political posturing, we have yet to reach a consensus of what to do with all of our waste. We wasted billions on one hole in the ground (which was a good hole, as far as holes go) only to be stopped dead cold by Senator Harry Reid. I would guess that Obama traded his support for health care for a stop cold card, but I don't know that for sure.

Politics aside, we have an issue that has to be dealt with. I suggest that we gather all of our fissionable material and nuclear waste along with our contaminated by-products and our nuclear warhead materials and bury them in Antarctica. Now listen before you gasp. I am not suggesting that we just bury it and forget about it. I am saying we build an installation a mile below the ice that will use this energy source to produce liquid hydrogen, that we then can pipe that stored energy north for use where we need it. By producing liquid hydrogen there and building pipelines north, we use the temperature of the planet to our advantage. (I am not even sure a system such as this will work, my point is to look for workable solutions instead of just creating more problems.)

I also suggest that we use the power created by the system to augment our failing magnetosphere. (Scientists tell us that our magnetosphere is weakening, why not enhance it while we still can? Or do we wait until the solar wind blows us off the planet?) We have this material, it's not going away, it's dangerous to the health of our families and future generations. We should use it for the good of all. I cannot tell you how to do it, but I know it can be done. That is why we have scientists, engineers, technicians and innovators. We can use more than just the immediately fissionable material, materials that have passed it's most efficient use in a nuclear power plant will continue to create large amounts of heat long after it has been removed. That material can be used to preheat water for turbines, or it can be used to heat the facility. I believe that everything that can be used, must be used if we are to survive. That is all I am going to say on that subject other than to say that we will be making a huge mistake if we just bury it in Yucca mountain and forget about it.

The military's of the world, or a drastically reduced complement of them, should be combined and start preparing for what is the inevitable threat to humanity. (According to the Drake equation, there are more than one intelligent species among the stars) If one of these species does ever decide to visit our planet, it will not be good for us. In our own history, whenever two civilizations meet, the least advanced culture is typically wiped out. (Always for it's resources!) I am not saying that little green men will show up tomorrow, what I am saying is that the world should prepare just in case. We all know (at least on a intellectual level) that it is possible. Would you rather fund an entity and it's science requirements (which will undoubtedly lead to advances) and not need them, or not have them and need them? It's the old condom question modified to the death of all humanity, isn't it?

If for example this threat showed up today, each country on the planet would want to respond in it's own manner. My country (the good ole- U. S. of A.) would attempt to bargain with them to gain a further technological advantage over the rest of humanity. If that failed them, they would destroy (or attempt to) said creatures and craft. Which would more than likely bring them down on the heads of everyone on the planet. Odds are that this is a threat that will never present itself and doesn't deserve further attention. Yet, one military to serve the planet is a given. Who knows, one day a population of formally content people may decide that they no longer like our world. They may discover a huge reserve of gold and decide that it belongs to them alone. We will always need a strong hand to deal with those who would take advantage of us all.

OK. say we keep a military and it decides to pull coup d'etat in order to rule us all, what would we do? We simply start deleting their digital selves. I cannot explain what that will mean to an individual in the very near future. (20 to 25 years in the capitalist world, 5 to 10 years in our new world.) The real constraint to a coup d'etat is in how our people are educated and treated. No one will desire power except within the confines of the "Chain of Councils" because it simply will not exist. We have all heard that power corrupts and absolute power corrupts absolutely. I have seen people with ridiculously small amounts of power (a cashier or security guard for example) try and use their power as a hammer rather than as a service, which it was originally given for. Sad!

Chapter 16 God and Religion

I realize that there are religious considerations to parts of this plan. The option of having your corpse eaten by beetles or having it turned into fuel are not exactly traditional. There is always a compromise to any situation. If we continue burying people in traditional cemeteries, we will run out of land long before we run out of bodies. I honestly think that to isolate your body from the circle of life is to truly die. Soon however, we will have the option of downloading our minds into a new digital universe. If the vessel we call our bodies is used up and is no longer needed, why do you care what happens to your corpse. I can hear you out there saying that God promised to raise you up to live again. If you truly believe in God, then you should know that he doesn't need a pile of bones or anything else to bring you back from the dead.

That doesn't mean that we shouldn't respect the wishes of the dead, but as an alternative to laying out bodies side by side and head to toe, we could drill deep holes in the earth and bury our dead in stacks. I am sure that families would want to be entombed together so who's to say that their headstone couldn't resemble a totem pole. Generation on top of generation, and the beautiful part of this is that a family could use the same "grave" for many generations. I know, I have gone to far for some of you, but do you not see the need? Or would you rather have graves spread across the planet leaving no room for the living?

Speaking of respect, that will have to become the underlying thread of our new world. Without respect of race, of religion, of community and of family, we will surely die. All of us are on this blue marble together. There is no way to separate yourself from the whole, even if you wanted to. This point reminds me of Israel or Palestine. Palestine insists on having a state of it's own. What they do not realize is that the do not need the rest of the world to tell them that they are a state. All they have to do is believe that they are a state. Two states, one land. Sounds simple enough to me. I outlined earlier how they can live together, they can actually build themselves out of the conflict. There will still be those who will not be happy no matter what. There will be those who will demand the destruction of the State of Israel, what they do not realize is, is that if they try to destroy the state, they have guaranteed the destruction of their own.

I don't believe that God will destroy us if we attempt to save ourselves, I could be wrong. To my mind, the destruction that is predicted in the Bible is a destruction of our own making. He doesn't have to destroy us, we are doing it for him. For a long time here in the U.S. there has been an underground movement of "survivalists," at least that's what we used to call them. Today they are called "preppers" as in to prepare to survive after we destroy ourselves. Oh ye of little faith. If we as a race (the human race) goes over the edge and destroys itself, there will be no surviving. All of the preparation in the world will not save you from his wrath.

There are those who pray for our destruction daily. It even says in the Bible that there will be those who pray for the day to come, but that they do not realize what horror that they wish upon themselves. I was guilty of this, except that I prayed that God would spare the earth and the creatures who make it home. I thought about our destruction for a long time until I realized that if we are destroyed, everything you ever loved will be destroyed along with it. It was at this time I also realized that God could destroy our world in the blink of an eye and bring it all back without us to corrupt it. Every squirrel can be remade and never miss a breath, never know the pain that is waiting for us. Yes, I know that the more I write, the more ammunition I give my detractors. So be it. I will give them plenty more before I am done.

Believing that we have are the "masters" of our world has brought us to the brink of destruction. The arrogance of it, to believe we are the masters of anything. There is an old saying that if you want to make God laugh, just tell him your plans. Even as I write, our lives are balanced upon the head of an unsteady pin. We can change that, we have to change that or we are done. It has never failed that throughout history every time we have thought that we are in control over a situation or a natural process, that arrogance has come back, like a wolf, to bite us in the ass. Keep that attitude up, it's worked so well for us so far.

If we have the strength to change our world and accept our neighbor as our brother, then we will have a chance. The "democratic" nations of the world merely pay lip service to the people. The veneer of that lie has worn so thin that even the government doesn't even repeat the lie anymore. Our governments serve the multinational corporations and in turn the men who control them. Nowhere on earth is free of the corporation. Strangely enough the corporation was originally founded to leverage the capital of the people allowing them to achieve goals that were out of the reach of the average man. They were created to serve the people. Somewhere along the way the world was turned on it's head.

Once we break away from oligarchic control and complete our singular consciousness, we will have created our salvation and our damnation all in one. I say that because there will be a singularity of consciousness. If we allow a few to control that, then we are doomed. If we are able to wrestle control of the system to serve ourselves and our families, then we will all share in the rewards. We have reached the point in history where we are able, through our technology, to live after our deaths. We have also reached the point in history that by perfecting this technology we risk the wrath of God. However, it just may be that the digital world is in fact the promised land. Our minds (and souls) will be able to live on in our digital worlds, streets literally paved in gold. I know, I know, how profane. Right? That's what you were thinking, wasn't it?

It may be that God has given us the ability to build our own "heaven." A technological universe where your mind can exist for as long as we can figure out how to power the system. It may be true, (It is true that energy nor matter can ever be destroyed, it merely changes states.) that the energy that makes us who we are stays together after our deaths and exists in some unknown state as a being. It may also be true that if we create these digital universes that to live in one for any length of time is equal to living in hell. We just don't know. I will tell you what we do know, we will build these systems. We will occupy them after the deaths of our physical selves. It is only a matter of time until our technology catches up to the level of our brains.

The scientists, engineers, technicians and innovators make great strides every day toward that goal. Once we release the world's information and allow everyone to work in a true open-source environment, we will reach those goals in a quarter of the time. Hence, within your lifetime, you will be able to download your mind into a digital universe. We may find that the information stored in our brains just isn't enough and that no matter how smart we are, the soul will leave us. I don't really know. We will try and every person on this planet will live two lives while they are alive. They will live in the physical world and in the digital world.

It may also be true that the first person who is fully downloaded into the system just might seize control of the entire system and make our digital lives hell. I say this because once we are able to live two lives in one, the digital life will feel just as real as our physical lives. If you go on a digital vacation,or any other adventure, the memories created by that experience will be just as real as stubbing your toe on the way to the bathroom.

What I have to cover, while I am on this subject is my belief in what God is. I believe that God is the sum total (plus much more) of all the consciousness of ALL living things. All life is a part of God, every leaf on every tree, every blade of grass, everything that is alive, has been alive or will ever be alive. God is a LIVING God. That is not to say that he isn't in the rocks of the earth or in the clouds that reflect the setting sun, because he is all of that too. The reason I bring this up, and I have said something to this effect before, is that once we combine all of our consciousnesses with/through our technology, we will have a glimpse of a reflection of God.

True democracy has often been called "mob rule" and said in such a way as to inspire fear and dread. How could the judgment of the entire world be anything less than right? We have been programed for so long to be consumers and to worship at the house of cheap plastic crap, that today, the total sum of the world's peoples thoughts will surely be skewed. But not wrong. There will be others among you who fear this way of life for fear that the majority of a population in India or China will be making decisions for you. That is just wrong, you are not looking at the "Chain of Councils" in a logical way. For those who question, let me spell it out for you one last time.

Your family, which will consist of your parents, your grandparents, your children etc, will make up the first line of council. You will decide for yourselves how you will live your lives within the bounds of the system set forth by your councils. Your family will select someone from your family to represent you and your interests in the community council. The community council will decide for itself how your community will be ruled, how your family and your community will live within the bounds of the system set forth by your councils. Your community council will elect a representative to represent your family and your community in the city or district council within the bounds of the system set forth by your councils. Your district council will elect a representative to serve your families, your communities and your district in the city councils to determine by what rules/laws your district will live by within the bounds of the system set forth by your councils. Your city councils will do the same for the county council, which will do the same for the state council. Your state council will do the same for your countries council and your countries council will do the same for your continent council.

Last but not least, your continent council will send their representative to serve your councils on the world council. I realize that this is a simplified version because we will have to decide on how to balance these councils so that one country or population of any particular demographic doesn't dominate any other council. For example in Israel there are six million Jews and two million Palestinians. There has to be a way to allow each demographic an equal say in how they live. The basic rule of our new system is to not exploiting one another. Do we give the Palestinians a plot of land and call it their own and then allow the Israelis to dominate them by virtue of numbers? Do we allow the Palestinians to allow emigration to the point to where their populations are balanced?

I don't believe that either of these is the answer, but I do believe that there is a solution. I have lived my life by my personal motto that, "There are no problems, only solutions." A pessimist sees nothing but obstacles, an optimist sees nothing but chances to grow, learn, innovate and solve. It is like another of my mottoes, "Attitude is everything." Both are true, if you start with the proper attitude, you can solve your way through any problem. I admit that the problems facing Israel and Palestine are not easily solved, but they can be solved because they are all human beings. I think in order to stop the violence that both parties should agree that if someone kills another in an act of "terror" then their families lives are forfeit. Sounds tough, but too often a family profits from the random slaying of innocence. Wouldn't you think twice before inflicting death and pain if you knew that your family would have to pay for it?

Once again, I have strayed off topic in a way. Back to God. Shouldn't we wait for our savior? God has given us a choice. Do you not believe that if a man had went to Noah and gotten on his knees and said, "Noah, I believe you, I believe that God is going to destroy our world. Would you allow me to humbly serve you and your family in return for sparing my life?" Do you think Noah would have turned him away?

Would God have turned him away? I cannot believe that God would have turned him aside if the man was sincere. If we wait to be saved without trying to save ourselves we are insuring our destruction. Surely he will save those who are worthy, but shouldn't they do their best to try and save those who are not? I am not saying that I am worthy, if it was up to me, I would be the first tossed to damnation.

This reminds me of a joke, not in the best of tastes, but it has a grain of truth in it. There is a man sitting on his roof in the middle of a flood. He prays to God to save him. About ten minutes later a boat comes along and offers him a ride, he turns it down saying, "No, God is going to save me." The boat leaves and the man continues to pray. About an hour later another boat arrives and offers to give the man a ride. Once again he says, "No, God is going to save me!" The second boat leaves and the man starts praying again. About four hours goes by before a helicopter flies over, stops to hover and offers the man a ride. For the third time he says, "No, God is going to save me!!!" The helicopter flies away. So, the man is sitting there and the sun has set and he is in the dark. He starts again with a new prayer, "God, why have you not saved me? Have I been bad? Is my faith lacking?" And out of the sky comes a voice like the rustling of leaves, "Just what do you want, I sent you two boats and a helicopter?"

We are like the man on the roof, we pray to be saved. We pray for the destruction of our "bad" neighbors. When all along we have the ability to save ourselves. This is what this entire text is about. We can change the world, we can go from a capitalist system that rapes our world to an economy of economy which will conserve our world. God provides if you only look. (No, I am not claiming to be a prophet. I am claiming to sum up all of the answers I have found when I looked for them. This didn't come to me in a dream or in a burning bush. Although there was a dream, but that was for me.) I say this because there will be those who claim that I am one thing or another. I am nothing more than a man who wants to see his family thrive and prosper for as many generations as have existed before me.

The resources of this planet are not infinite, as they dwindle our situation becomes more and more precarious. Seven billion mouths wanting to be fed and watered each and every day. The U.N. Declaration for Human Rights says that you have the right to live a decent life, to have a decent meal, to have clean water. The problem with that is that the people who decided that you have those rights think that they are the responsibility of the someone else. Not their responsibility. The U.N. itself is a problem because it exists to legitimize the existence of the Nation State. We can use their declaration, we cannot use them. None of them. There is not one among them who wouldn't deny you a decent life if it meant that they would have to use their resources to provide it. Remember that. We can only take care of each other, because our countries and nations will not take care of us.

Here in the U.S. we call our Civil War the war where brother fought brother, where son fought father. It did divide our loyalties, that I do not deny. Every war in history has been fought between brothers. Have we ever had the social maturity to see it for that before now. We are of different colors, different nations, different religions, different ideologies, but we are all human beings. It is the one defining factor, the only factor that means anything. It is easy to point out our differences, what separates us, what divides us. It is even easier to demonize each other so that killing each other is like killing a rabid dog rather than a human brother.

Scientists (through the study of DNA and by world wide sampling) have come to the conclusion that we are all descended from four women. You could say that their great-great-great grandmother was Eve. They concluded that during one of the ice ages (75,000 years ago) that our race was nearly extinct and that a genetic bottleneck was created at that time reducing the worlds population to somewhere between 6,000 and 15,000 people. The system they used to deduced that number is beyond me, but when they went back further (140,000 to 200,000 years ago) they can pinpoint one mother of all of us, a Mother whom they call Mitochondrial Eve.

We are all one large family, throughout the tens of thousands of years we have divided up, developed distinctive traits, developed distinctive looks, developed distinct cultures, distinct rituals and a distinctive sets of beliefs. Seems almost impossible that nearly every culture came to the same conclusion that there is only one God. That they all came to that conclusion about the same time in history even though there was limited contact between these cultures. In some cases these cultures had no contact between one another (at least there is no proof of contact) in any historical record.

To summarize my point, God has given us the tools to insure our salvation. We can save every human, every animal, every fish, every tree and blade of grass. We can save our little blue marble. Even if we cannot save it, why would we not try? It's not a question of what God you believe in. It's not a question of what race you belong to. It's not a question of your political beliefs. It's not a question of what social class you belong to. It is a question of do you want your family to survive, to prosper, to have security and a clean healthy environment. If even once you decided that you cannot be a part of the change because you don't want to save another party, religion or race, then you have damned your family and yourself by your own bias.

Chapter 17 Goals

Our goals as a "one world family" have to be investigated
and defined by a group of scientists, engineers, technicians
and innovators with more experience and knowledge than I
have. In a very short period of time as that is the one thing
that we are lacking. Anything as a civilization is possible
provided that we are willing to spend our political will. Cash
(as it is now defined) is a useless commodity. Our true wealth,
i.e. what we actually have to spend to accomplish our goals is
our time (resource credits) and our resources. I will outline
those items that I believe have to be addressed immediately
along with ideas that I have that may help along the way.
Without a doubt one of our first goals will be to slow, then
reverse the trend of global warming. (Hard to believe in
global warming or climate change when it's twenty degrees

outside.)

One of the first steps which we have to take is to build the energy system I outlined in the "Energy" chapter. We cannot quit our oil addiction cold turkey, the pain it would inflict on our people would be too great to bear. With that said, the slow reduction of oil will be possible as our clean energy systems come online. While working on this clean energy conversion we must convert our gasoline burning vehicles to hydrogen powered vehicles. The production of hydrogen is not an energy source in itself but rather an energy storage medium. Every ounce of power produced that is not used is wasted due to our lack of ability to store that energy. Each milliamp of power not used should be converted to hydrogen storage.

Every ounce of urine in the world should be saved and used for conversion to hydrogen. (It takes one third the power to convert urine to hydrogen than it does to convert water to hydrogen.) At the same time, we need to save every gram of phosphates from urine for use as fertilizer. (Our natural reserves of it become lower every day.) I realize that it sounds disgusting, but we are talking about resource production using

ONE THIRD of the energy to produce. Once our clean energy production facilities are online in the ocean, we can use all of that power by producing hydrogen in off peak hours. The goal on the back end would be to stop burning coal (there is no such thing as clean coal.) along with oil and natural gas. You will hear people say that it is not possible to produce the electricity needed to keep our world moving without oil, those are the naysayers. What we lack in electrical production capacity can be purchased with political will. It is not a lack of technology nor is it a lack of resources, it is a lack of willpower.

We have engineered our planet for the last two centuries, although without realizing it and not in our favor. We can purposely engineer the planet to repair the damage done to the earth. While we work on reducing the amount of carbon dioxide that we release into the atmosphere, we can also work on carbon capture systems. Whether they are graphene based filters or we capture it at the source of release, we need to make huge gains on this front. We also have to conceive or invent a way to store this carbon dioxide in a way that it will never be re released. There is a way to store, compress and harden carbon dioxide turning it into stone products which can be used for sidewalks, curbs and other items typically made with stone.

I am sure that there are other innovative ways to capture and store or recycle this resource (because that is exactly what it is) that none of us have even considered yet. I have heard tale of a system that allows for the production of jet fuels etc through the combination of captured carbon dioxide along with hydrogen. I see no reason we could not use this method so long as we maintain a resource neutral system. (Meaning that we capture or store more CO_2 than we release into the environment and maintain a net negative.)

Besides having a carbon dioxide problem on the planet, we have a plastics problem on the planet. There is plastic everywhere, we have to clean it up. I envision thousands of solar powered drift boats that zigzags across our oceans skimming plastics. These drift boats will seek out their mother ships once they are full, offload and go back to work. The plastics collected by this system will be melted down into cubes for use on the billion and a half homes we have to build.

In the same family of our drift boats, I also can picture thousands upon thousands of solar powered oxygen boats that will roam the dead zones of our oceans. These oxygen boats will not only skim off the algae blooms, but they will also pump oxygen to the depths of the oceans so that sea life may take hold in these dead areas once again. The algae that is skimmed off will be brought to a mother-ship, collected and converted into bio fuels. Why waste a resource that we have created on accident.

While we are still on the water, we will create a series of larger filter boats that will prowl our rivers. These boats (or fixed islands along the rivers) will have the job of filtering nitrogen and phosphorus out of the water until we can build our self-sustaining farms. Once our new farms are completed, they will be able to capture all of their own chemicals used for growth. If we can capture a third of the chemicals that escape the farms in the mid west alone the numbers would be astronomical. (It's hard to find data on the amount of runoff from the mid-west, the numbers that I was able to find amount to 2.1 billion pounds of nitrogen and 375 million pounds of phosphorus. These numbers were said to be 34% lower nitrogen losses and 46% lower phosphorus losses than previous estimates.) http://farmfutures.com/blogs-epa-re-write-midwest-runoff-regs-7672

I have to believe that we can do better than that. Is it any wonder that the amount of dead zones in the world has risen from a known one in 1950 to close to 500 today. With dead zones ranging in size from half a kilometer square to being larger than the State of New Jersey. Really? What exactly has to happen before the people of the world stand up and say, "NO MORE!" Does half the world have to burn? I honestly believe that a minimum of one billion people would have to die before anyone cared. And then it would have to be the "right people" before anyone who could do anything cared. I CARE NOW!!!! If you want even half a hope in hell of saving our planet, you damn well better start caring now.

To continue, if what I told you in the last paragraph doesn't tick you off, then we are screwed. Recycling is a given. Except instead of only 80% of people doing partial recycling and 25% of people not recycling at all, all of us

WILL recycle everything. Wet garbage will stay at home and go into a mulch pile. Aluminum, glass and cardboard will be recycled as those are easy. The problem materials are everything else and for that I have an answer.

At each trash collection site (where most trash is collected in the U.S.) we will install machines that will accept every type of non-recyclable and non-wet garbage. (Plastics are a huge recycling problem due to the fact that plastic products are made from multiple materials.) These machines will accept all types of plastics in one side and everything else in the other. It will compress the non-plastic trash and encase it in the conglomerated plastic from it's shredder side. These blocks will be interlocking and capable of being used in the construction of the billion and a half homes we have to build.

Until such time as we can stop the manufacture of plastics made from petrochemicals. There are many alternatives to petrochemical plastics currently on the market. Plastics made from petrochemicals have an uncanny ability to attract PCB's along with a myriad of other toxic chemicals to themselves especially in our oceans and waterways. We no longer need these plastics except for in rare occasions. I could go into all of the harm that they cause, but I am sure one of the many plastic manufactures would feel the need to sue me. Oh, hell. Who cares, let the SOB's sue me!

The need for limited petrochemical based plastics will be highly restricted and regulated. Whenever they are used they will be required to be one hundred percent recycled or reused. We do not need anymore toxins leached into our soils or our groundwater. This brings up a related product, rubber for tires. Were you aware that the tire manufactures of the world could have produced a tire that would last for the practical life span of a vehicle? I could say that they will be required to manufacture tires to meet that spec, however, since they will no longer exist as separate entities and I am not sure of just what our mass transportation system will look like, I will say this.

Tires manufactured for our collective use vehicles (we cannot crush all the worlds gas burners, it would be a crime, but we can save some for recreation use by vacationers etc) will last as long as a tire can be made to last. We are tired (pun intended) of purchasing the same products over and over again when it isn't necessary. It is nothing more than a waste of resources. In a bid to keep an ever demanding consumer base, every manufacture on the planet has designed their products to ultimately fail, it's just wrong.

My other point concerning tires are the billions of them spread across the planet and buried in landfills. Those tires (which are a form of resource) can be reduced to a resin and mixed with asphalt to use as building blocks for the billions of homes we need to build. Or they can be used in the same manner as they are used in the "spaceship earth" housing in the desert southwest. These tires are staggered and packed with earth to make retaining walls along with regular walls for sustainable housing. How they are eventually used will be up to the scientific guys to figure out, I am just making suggestions here.

I considered line itemizing every product or group of products and suggesting how and why they could be made better, along with the reason behind it. Once I thought it over I decided that I have done the real work with forming a blueprint to save the planet. I have to admit that not even a third of the ideas in this text are my own. The true visionaries did the hard work long ago. I wish that I could remember their names and reference them individually. That is not possible for I have been reading everything I could get my hands on for over thirty years. I have no idea where some of these ideas originated. The one idea that I will claim for myself is the energy production systems. That's all mine. I even tried to sell that to the green energy companies until I came upon a realization. The energy companies of the world know that it is possible to create clean renewable energy without the need for hydrocarbons. They know this, but if they were to develop it, you wouldn't want to pay those thousand dollar a month electric bills.

The people of this world are capable of designing and building anything that's needed for them to survive. Once we open-source all information, watch out, we will build our self sustaining world in no time. In it we will have all of the modern conveniences that we have become accustom to, along with some we haven't comprehended yet. We will also have our DS (digital selves) which will allow us to take that next step in evolution within the next decade. (surprise-surprise) We will also have any number of digital universes to play in. What will be astonishing about the digital world is that you will not be able to tell the difference between inside and out without a series of markers that only you are aware of so that you will know if you're in the physical or digital world. Some might say that you could just look real close, but to their dismay, the real world becomes pix-elated just like the digital world when you get down to the small stuff. Weird huh?

Chapter 18 Future

I want to lay out a glimpse of the future for you just in case we survive capitalism. Where can we go and what can we do? When we get past the point of securing the world for everyone, we will have an inexhaustible amount of human capital that we can spend in any number of ways. We can work toward understanding and manipulating gravity and space-time. (We cannot work on one without the other!) We can build an elevator into space. (totally possible) We can build fusion drives, solar sails a quarter of the size of the moon. Anything that will further the goals and dreams of the human race will be within our grasp.

The fact that we will have created a digital universe and will be able to download ourselves into a server will open the heavens to us. There will be no need to send live humans out into the cold regions of space. Time will mean nothing to those of us who have been downloaded, this means that we can build a series of ships and launch tens of thousands of humans (their consciousnesses anyway) out to explore the habitable planets that we have discovered. Because there is no need to preserve a physical life, these ships will cost less, be lighter and they will be able to travel for hundreds of thousands of light years before reaching their destinations. Once a "group" of humans arrive at a suitable planet, they can download themselves into a robotic avatar and with the help of a little chemistry they can synthesize DNA and bring physical humans to life.

It's all in the realm of possibility, unless we fail to wrestle control from the rapists of our world. I find it humorous that sci-fi movies often depict an alien race coming to our planet in an attempt to deplete our resources before moving on. Imagine how pissed those aliens will be if they arrive fifty years from now and find the planet already stripped? (if we fail that is) We cannot afford to fail. This isn't just your life and mine on the line, this is every generation from here on out who is in danger. We all have to agree on the best way to proceed. The possibilities to advance our race are endless. The multinationals scream constantly about regulation and oversight, we will not be able to leash them unless we take them over and beat them like red headed step children. I know, I know.

A lot of what I have put in this text is controversial simply because I believe in punishment. Let me tell you, my father believed in punishment and even though I would have been diagnosed with A.D.D. or some other alphabet soup disorder today, I stayed in line. The children of today are unruly because they lack discipline. Plain and simple. Our society and civilization have the same issues for the same reason. To repair this dysfunction we do two things, we make most things legal and the perverted killer stuff punishable by death. Simple! Not the thirty years on death row with cheesecake on Thursday type of death sentence either.

This is one point that I don't think I can make enough, if you're found guilty of raping a fifteen year old girl, (or anyone) the father has the option of killing you himself (upon announcement of the verdict) or he can have a proxy do it for him. If you are convicted of murder, same deal. If you enslave a fellow human, well we went over that didn't we? Trust me, you wouldn't want to be in that position if I was the proxy. I wouldn't even blink, then I would go home, have a nice supper and sleep like a baby. See, fixed. I will say one last thing, in cases where someone has to be incarcerated, they should be under the jurisdiction of the mental health authorities. Our prison system is full of either non-violent offenders or the mentally deficient. If we changed our current system from a profit based detention system to a mental health treatment system we could cut recidivism in half. (those mental health guys and their electric shocks can sway the strongest of wills.)

Who am I?

Allow me to introduce myself, I am Leonard R. Goodwin II. Born in Cookeville, Tennessee on July 7, 1968. Like most American's I identify myself with what I do. I am a Master Carpenter, Author, Philosopher, Historian, Cartographer, Foreman, Superintendent, Field Engineer, Set Builder, Set Carpenter, Husband, Father, Brother, Son and most importantly of all, I am a Human Being.

I am proud of the last name, Goodwin, there are many variations of the name. If you go back about 42 generations ago you will find that my great (x42) grandfather was the last Anglo-Saxon King of Britain and lost that crown along with his life at the Battle of Hastings. We Goodwin's have been at almost all of the great turning points in history. To name a few, the first little girl to point a finger and call a woman witch at Salem was a little Goodwin girl. Mary Shelley's step-father, to whom she dedicated the book Frankenstein was a Goodwin. Edward the Confessor's wife was Edith Goodwin. My family goes back to the beginning of recorded history on the Isle of Britain. I don't even have to mention the most famous historian of our times. I will how ever mention my cousin (who is not a Goodwin) Al Gore Jr. former Vice-President. (If my family wasn't involved, our relatives were.) Even in England to this day, the Goodwin name is well known. (wont go there) We have been in the U.S. since long before there was a U.S. We have fought in every major war that the U.S. has been involved in since it's inception, including the French and Indian war which predates America.

Now that I have told you all of that, I have to say that it means precisely nothing. I am just another guy who puts his socks on one at a time. I have one son, one daughter (both are grown) and two grandsons, thought I would throw that in for good measure. I will say that I got the working title from my cousins movie, "An Inconvenient Truth", which is why my working title was, "An Intelligent Answer." One of the things I find disturbing by that documentary and many others, is that they all outline a problem without a solution.

I would like to acknowledge Buckminster Fuller who I quoted in this text. The quote, "Our current system is only capable of taking care of 43% of the worlds population while leaving the other 57% out in the cold to starve." was taken directly from him. He was ahead of his time and I have no doubt that if his time was now, he would be writing a text very much like this one.

Throughout this text, you will note that I have not called it a book nor a novel nor a short story because it is a text. It isn't long enough to be a book nor short enough to be an article. It is what it is.

One last note and I am done. I sincerely hope that I have gotten through to at least a few of you. I hope that we can save our planet for future generations. I am only charging $2.00 for this text because my cut will be a few cents over two resource credits. It is my hope that everyone on the planet will read this text. If I make anything on it at all, you can be sure that I will use those funds for the betterment of my family and my community. If we don't help each other, well do I really have to say it again? If you would like to respond, buildermaker@live.com

U.N. Declaration of Human Rights follows this page, please read the inherent hypocrisy. Rampant, not implied. We, accept the rights declared in the aforementioned Declaration. We respectfully disavow the right of the "Nation State" to exist.

Addendum

This text was copied exactly from the U.N.'s web page, there have been no changes or additions made.

PREAMBLE

Whereas recognition of the inherent dignity and of the equal and inalienable rights of all members of the human family is the foundation of freedom, justice and peace in the world,

Whereas disregard and contempt for human rights have resulted in barbarous acts which have outraged the conscience of mankind, and the advent of a world in which human beings shall enjoy freedom of speech and belief and freedom from fear and want has been proclaimed as the highest aspiration of the common people,

Whereas it is essential, if man is not to be compelled to have recourse, as a last resort, to rebellion against tyranny and oppression, that human rights should be protected by the rule of law,

Whereas it is essential to promote the development of friendly relations between nations,

Whereas the peoples of the United Nations have in the Charter reaffirmed their faith in fundamental human rights, in the dignity and worth of the human person and in the equal rights of men and women and have determined to promote social progress and better standards of life in larger freedom,

Whereas Member States have pledged themselves to achieve, in co-operation with the United Nations, the promotion of universal respect for and observance of human rights and fundamental freedoms,

Whereas a common understanding of these rights and freedoms is of the greatest importance for the full realization of this pledge,

Now, Therefore THE GENERAL ASSEMBLY proclaims THIS UNIVERSAL DECLARATION OF HUMAN RIGHTS as a common standard of achievement for all peoples and all nations, to the end that every individual and every organ of society, keeping this Declaration constantly in mind, shall strive by teaching and education to promote respect for these rights and freedoms and by progressive measures, national and international, to secure their universal and effective recognition and observance, both among the peoples of Member States themselves and among the peoples of territories under their jurisdiction.

lArticle 1.

lAll human beings are born free and equal in dignity and rights. They are endowed with reason and conscience and should act towards one another in a spirit of brotherhood.

lArticle 2.

lEveryone is entitled to all the rights and freedoms set forth in this Declaration, without distinction of any kind, such as race, colour, sex, language, religion, political or other opinion, national or social origin, property, birth or other status. Furthermore, no distinction shall be made on the basis of the political, jurisdictional or international status of the country or territory to which a person belongs, whether it be independent, trust, non-self-governing or under any other limitation of sovereignty.

lArticle 3.

lEveryone has the right to life, liberty and security of person.

lArticle 4.

lNo one shall be held in slavery or servitude; slavery and the slave trade shall be prohibited in all their forms.

lArticle 5.

lNo one shall be subjected to torture or to cruel, inhuman or degrading treatment or punishment.

lArticle 6.

lEveryone has the right to recognition everywhere as a person before the law.

lArticle 7.

lAll are equal before the law and are entitled without any discrimination to equal protection of the law. All are entitled to equal protection against any discrimination in violation of this Declaration and against any incitement to such discrimination.

lArticle 8.

lEveryone has the right to an effective remedy by the competent national tribunals for acts violating the fundamental rights granted him by the constitution or by law.

IArticle 9.

INo one shall be subjected to arbitrary arrest, detention or exile.

IArticle 10.

IEveryone is entitled in full equality to a fair and public hearing by an independent and impartial tribunal, in the determination of his rights and obligations and of any criminal charge against him.

IArticle 11.

I(1) Everyone charged with a penal offence has the right to be presumed innocent until proved guilty according to law in a public trial at which he has had all the guarantees necessary for his defence.

I(2) No one shall be held guilty of any penal offence on account of any act or omission which did not constitute a penal offence, under national or international law, at the time when it was committed. Nor shall a heavier penalty be imposed than the one that was applicable at the time the penal offence was committed.

lArticle 12.

lNo one shall be subjected to arbitrary interference with his privacy, family, home or correspondence, nor to attacks upon his honour and reputation. Everyone has the right to the protection of the law against such interference or attacks.

lArticle 13.

l(1) Everyone has the right to freedom of movement and residence within the borders of each state.

l(2) Everyone has the right to leave any country,

including his own, and to return to his country.

lArticle 14.

l(1) Everyone has the right to seek and to enjoy in other countries asylum from persecution.

l(2) This right may not be invoked in the case of prosecutions genuinely arising from non-political crimes or from acts contrary to the purposes and principles of the United Nations.

lArticle 15.

l(1) Everyone has the right to a nationality.

l(2) No one shall be arbitrarily deprived of his nationality nor denied the right to change his nationality.

lArticle 16.

l(1) Men and women of full age, without any limitation due to race, nationality or religion, have the right to marry and to found a family. They are entitled to equal rights as to marriage, during marriage and at its dissolution.

l(2) Marriage shall be entered into only with the free and full consent of the intending spouses.

l(3) The family is the natural and fundamental group unit of society and is entitled to protection by society and the State.

lArticle 17.

l(1) Everyone has the right to own property alone as well as in association with others.

l(2) No one shall be arbitrarily deprived of his property.

lArticle 18.

Everyone has the right to freedom of thought, conscience and religion; this right includes freedom to change his religion or belief, and freedom, either alone or in community with others and in public or private, to manifest his religion or belief in teaching, practice, worship and observance.

Article 19.

Everyone has the right to freedom of opinion and expression; this right includes freedom to hold opinions without interference and to seek, receive and impart information and ideas through any media and regardless of frontiers.

Article 20.

(1) Everyone has the right to freedom of peaceful assembly and association.

(2) No one may be compelled to belong to an association.

Article 21.

(1) Everyone has the right to take part in the government of his country, directly or through freely chosen representatives.

(2) Everyone has the right of equal access to public service in his country.

(3) The will of the people shall be the basis of the authority of government; this will shall be expressed in periodic and genuine elections which shall be by universal and equal suffrage and shall be held by secret vote or by equivalent free voting procedures.

Article 22.

Everyone, as a member of society, has the right to social security and is entitled to realization, through national effort and international co-operation and in accordance with the organization and resources of each State, of the economic, social and cultural rights indispensable for his dignity and the free development of his personality.

lArticle 23.

l(1) Everyone has the right to work, to free choice of employment, to just and favourable conditions of work and to protection against unemployment.

l(2) Everyone, without any discrimination, has the right to equal pay for equal work.

l(3) Everyone who works has the right to just and favourable remuneration ensuring for himself and his family an existence worthy of human dignity, and supplemented, if necessary, by other means of social protection.

l(4) Everyone has the right to form and to join trade unions for the protection of his interests.

lArticle 24.

Everyone has the right to rest and leisure, including reasonable limitation of working hours and periodic holidays with pay.

Article 25.

(1) Everyone has the right to a standard of living adequate for the health and well-being of himself and of his family, including food, clothing, housing and medical care and necessary social services, and the right to security in the event of unemployment, sickness, disability, widowhood, old age or other lack of livelihood in circumstances beyond his control.

(2) Motherhood and childhood are entitled to special care and assistance. All children, whether born in or out of wedlock, shall enjoy the same social protection.

Article 26.

(1) Everyone has the right to education. Education

shall be free, at least in the elementary and fundamental stages. Elementary education shall be compulsory. Technical and professional education shall be made generally available and higher education shall be equally accessible to all on the basis of merit.

l(2) Education shall be directed to the full development of the human personality and to the strengthening of respect for human rights and fundamental freedoms. It shall promote understanding, tolerance and friendship among all nations, racial or religious groups, and shall further the activities of the United Nations for the maintenance of peace.

l(3) Parents have a prior right to choose the kind of education that shall be given to their children.

lArticle 27.

l(1) Everyone has the right freely to participate in

the cultural life of the community, to enjoy the arts
and to share in scientific advancement and its
benefits.

I(2) Everyone has the right to the protection of the
moral and material interests resulting from any
scientific, literary or artistic production of which he is
the author.

IArticle 28.

IEveryone is entitled to a social and international order
in which the rights and freedoms set forth in this
Declaration can be fully realized.

IArticle 29.

I(1) Everyone has duties to the community in
which alone the free and full development of his
personality is possible.

I(2) In the exercise of his rights and freedoms,

everyone shall be subject only to such limitations as are determined by law solely for the purpose of securing due recognition and respect for the rights and freedoms of others and of meeting the just requirements of morality, public order and the general welfare in a democratic society.

l(3) These rights and freedoms may in no case be exercised contrary to the purposes and principles of the United Nations.

lArticle 30.

lNothing in this Declaration may be interpreted as implying for any State, group or person any right to engage in any activity or to perform any act aimed at the destruction of any of the rights and freedoms set forth herein.

www.ingramcontent.com/pod-product-compliance
Lightning Source LLC
Chambersburg PA
CBHW060459290526
45791CB00001B/191